DREAMS OF HEAVEN

Praise for DREAMS OF HEAVEN

"*Dreams of Heaven* compels you to examine your beliefs about life and death. You will be drawn to read every page."
— Reverend Emile Gauvreau, Center for Spiritual Living Cape Coral

"The book is like an epiphanous dream probing the mysteries of birth, life, and death. It is one of those gems of spiritual literature that becomes a permanent fixture in our lives, always remembered as a gift for that special friend with whom we wish to share our most deeply felt beliefs."
— Hal Zina Bennett, Ph.D., best-selling author of *Write From the Heart* and *Follow Your Bliss*

"A great read for anyone ready to heal and wake up."
— Alex Marchand, author of *The Universe Is a Dream: The Secrets of Existence Revealed*

"The love just radiates from the story. The love of a mother for her family and her love for Jesus. This love extends to the reader. *Dreams of Heaven* is simply beautiful. It will soothe your soul. It will speak to your heart. It will fill you with hope. I loved it."
— Julia Wilson, Christian Bookaholic

"*Dreams of Heaven* is soul food that gives rise to questions about our definitions of reality, time and love. A beautifully told, elegantly spun story of the soul, as well as a master teacher and guide through changes."
— Veronica O'Grady, Light Leaders International

"A truly memorable read."
— Viking Reviews

"Reading this book made me feel light and free. I highly recommend it."
— Pat Luboff, Underrated Reads

"One of the most wonderful stories that I have ever read. I highly recommend this book to everyone!"
— Bonnie Cehovet, book reviewer

"*Dreams of Heaven* by Elizabeth M. Herrera is a beautiful heartfelt book on trusting inner guidance, the power of dreams, the reality of spirit, true love and the eternal gift of life that lives beyond our physical connections and beyond our physical existence. Herrera's book profoundly reminds us that 'what is immortal can never die.'"
— Andrea R. Garrison, host/producer of Online With Andrea, and author of *The Crossing Over of Mattie Pearl*

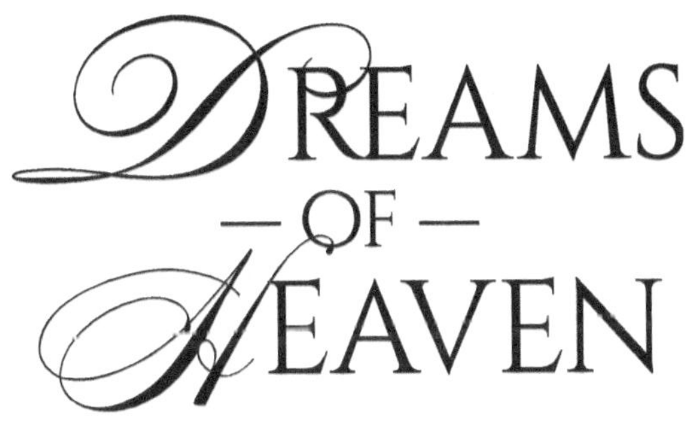

DREAMS OF HEAVEN

Elizabeth M. Herrera

BLUE GATOR

*Dedicated to my husband, daughter and son,
who remind me each day how precious life is.*

Preface

THE IDEA FOR THIS story came in a vivid dream where Jesus Christ appeared and showed me four scenes and nothing else. When I woke up, I knew I would write this story, but it wasn't an easy task. I had no idea how the scenes would connect or how the story would unfold. Each writing session involved me sitting quietly, listening to the inspiration, and letting the words flow.

My gift from this process was to see how I resisted the information that presented itself. The process also involved the release of my fears. When I finally listened without hesitation, the words flowed like divine ink, covering the pages and opening my heart.

For those with a Christian background, *Dreams of Heaven* will defy your traditional notion of Jesus' teachings 2,000 years ago. I can only say to you, "Listen with your heart and enjoy a story interpreted through love."

Blessings,
Elizabeth M. Herrera

ACKNOWLEDGMENTS

My husband, Jon Phillips, for his support.

Janet Harvey-Clark and Ian McKenzie-Vincent
for their editing.

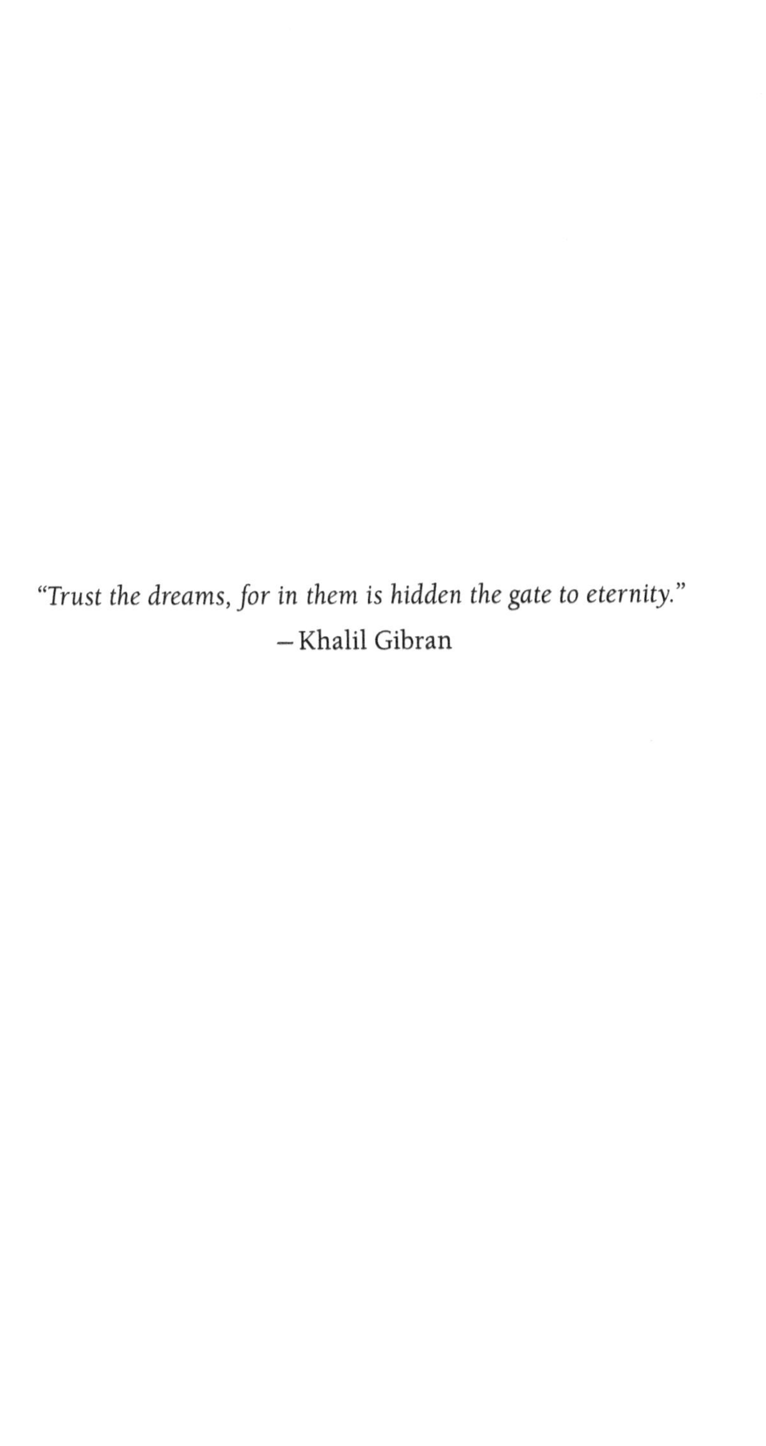

"Trust the dreams, for in them is hidden the gate to eternity."
— Khalil Gibran

CHAPTER 1

The Accident

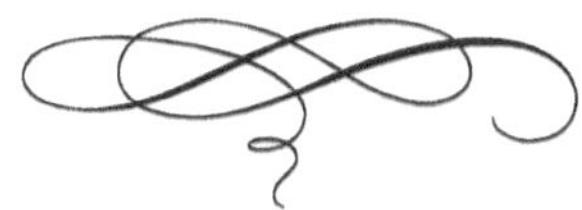

POLICE CARS AND AMBULANCES were parked haphazardly along a desolate stretch of Highway 50 near the North Carolina coastline. Flashing red and blue lights filled the night and reflected on the rain-covered asphalt. The pulsating lights were occasionally interrupted by the rescuers whose actions lacked urgency. There was no hurry. Those in the SUV were presumed dead, although the official declaration was still pending.

With rain dripping off his black metal helmet and yellow reflective rain gear, a firefighter inserted a mechanical jaw into the seam of the impacted passenger door to start the process of prying it open. He turned on the machine. Its growling metal jaws expanded. The vehicle's mangled steel, unwilling to change yet again so soon, slowly yielded, emitting a loud high-pitched squeal. "Grab it," he instructed.

Two grim-faced firefighters took hold of the twisted metal with gloved hands, pulling with determined effort. The door finally gave way, exposing the gruesome scene inside.

The mother was slumped against the seat. Blood ran down her face. Her legs were trapped beneath the glove box. The father sat in the driver's seat, his head pressed against the shattered side window. In the back seat, the boy and teenage girl's arms and legs were entangled.

A paramedic checked the mother for signs of life, pressing his fingers against her neck, but, as expected, found none. He stepped back.

Police officer Nolan came over, asking the paramedic, "Any luck, Jack?"

"Nope. Tragic. Just tragic."

The police officer solemnly nodded in agreement. "I found the family dog in the ditch over there. What a shame—all the way around."

The medical examiner approached them. He was a tall older man with thinning gray hair. Without saying a word, he snapped on latex gloves, then reached inside the wreckage to feel the passenger's limp cool wrist. Not finding a detectable pulse, he leaned in further.

The woman's glazed eyes stared back at him. He was uncomfortably close to her inside the cramped wreckage. He shone a penlight over her pupils looking for any sign of brain activity.

Suddenly, the woman arched her back, gasping for a breath.

The startled medical examiner lurched backwards, hitting his head on the door jam. He winced, then scrambled out of the vehicle. "She's alive!" he yelled excitedly.

The paramedic shifted into high gear, shouting at his partner who was unloading a gurney from the back of the ambulance, "Bring the trauma bag!"

CHAPTER 2

Bad Dreams

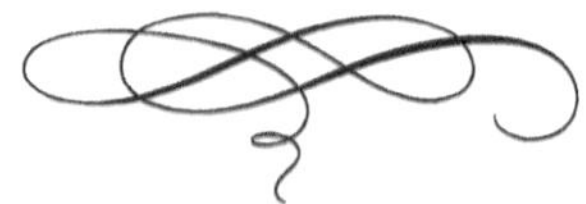

SAVANNAH BOLTED UPRIGHT IN bed, shaking from a bad dream. It took her a moment to realize she was safe in her own bedroom. Relief flooded over her, but her heart kept pounding. She glanced at her sleeping husband before getting up, grabbing her robe from the foot of the bed.

She left the bedroom, heading down the dark stairwell, reaching the living room decorated with rattan furniture that mimicked the tropics. The overhead palm-leaf fan slowly spun.

Savannah pulled open the sliding glass door. The sea breeze rushed past her, rustling the vertical blinds. She stepped outside, moving across the deck. The ocean roared. She stood by the railing, watching the waves ebb and flow under the moon's glow. The salty mist settled over her, layer by layer, slowly creating a vaporous cocoon. Savannah didn't mind the dampness. It made her feel connected—like an old house being overcome by the elements, metamorphosing back to its natural state. In the distance, thunder rumbled. A storm was brewing.

Someone opened the sliding glass door, startling Savannah who turned to see her husband, Steve, coming towards her.

He reached her side, asking, "What are you doing out here?"

"Just getting some fresh air."

Steve didn't believe her. "Something wrong?"

Savannah appreciated his concern, however, thinking about the nightmare sent shivers down her spine. Not wanting to talk about it, she replied, "Oh, it's nothing."

"Are you sure?"

She faced the water to avoid his gaze.

Steve kept looking at her, hoping she would confide in him. When she didn't answer, he became concerned, asking, "What is it? Do you feel okay?"

"Yes, I'm fine. It was just a bad dream. That's all."

"A dream? What was it about?"

"You don't want to hear about it. Trust me."

"I can handle it."

"Fine. I don't remember the first part, but the dream began with a car accident." She was surprised at the intensity of her emotions as she recounted the details. Her breathing grew labored. "All of us were in the SUV. There were lights and ambulances everywhere. The worst part is..." she hesitated before saying, "you and the kids were killed."

Steve's gut tightened. His wife's fear was contagious. He fought against it, reminding himself, *Dreams aren't real*. His rational mind took control and he calmly responded, "We're all fine. Like you said, 'It was just a dream.'"

"I know," she agreed, but truthfully she was worried the dream was more than that. She feared it was a premonition.

He consoled her, "I once read that when you dream about someone dying, it really means your relationship is changing. Maybe you're afraid of the kids getting older and leaving the nest."

"Maybe," she replied, even though the explanation didn't feel right to her.

Steve wrapped his arm around her, pulling her closer. Together, they watched the indigo waves pitch to a primordial rhythm.

Savannah wanted to claim this moment, hoping that

somehow she could stop the approaching black train that bore an ominous warning. In the distance, she heard it rumbling down the tracks. A long shrill whistle drifted through the air, coming closer and closer until it crossed the divide between realities, whispering in her ear, "I'm coming."

CHAPTER 3

Emergency Room

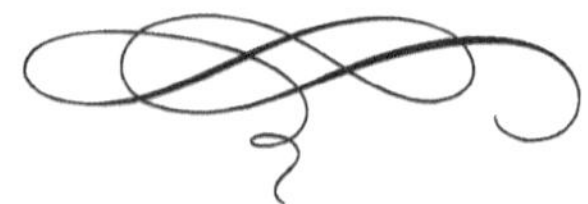

CAROL, A WOMAN IN her mid-60s, and her grown daughter, Jennifer, rushed out of the lit parking lot and into the emergency room, making a beeline to the admissions office.

Gripping the counter, Carol blurted, "I got a call that my son and his family were in a car accident. Where do we go? How do we see them?"

The receptionist was sympathetic. "Let me check. Name of the patients, please."

"Steve and Savannah Watson. And their kids, Justin and Emily."

The woman typed in the names, then waited for the results. Her expression became guarded. "It appears the doctors are working on this case at the moment. But I've noted that you are here, and as soon as they can, they'll come out to give you an update. Okay? You can wait here in the lobby."

Carol pressured the receptionist, "Can you at least tell me how they are?"

"Sorry, ma'am, only the doctors can do that. Please have a seat. I promise, they will let you know as soon as they can."

Herman Gomez, an older short-statured man, walked into the lobby looking like he had been asleep when he got the call.

Carol spotted her son's father-in-law, waving to him and calling out, "Herman! Over here."

After they hugged, he asked her, "What's going on? Are they okay?"

"I don't know yet. The receptionist said the doctors would let us know, hopefully soon."

Herman nodded, then noticed Carol's daughter. They gave each other an obligatory hug.

At a loss for words, the three of them sat down to wait for the news.

A few minutes later, an ER doctor appeared. He had put on a fresh lab coat to cover the blood on his green scrubs. He looked worn out as he asked them, "Are you with the Watson family?"

The three of them nodded.

"I'm Doctor Williams. There are some matters I need to discuss with you. Could you follow me, please?" He led them to a small communal office, holding the door open until everyone was inside. "Please, have a seat," he requested. There were only three chairs so he remained standing, leaning on the edge of the empty metal desk.

Herman nervously cleared his throat. "Please, just tell us how they're doing."

Before the doctor could answer, there was a knock on the door. A nurse peeked her head in, saying, "Someone's here for the Watson family." She stepped back to allow a woman with mascara running down her face to enter the room.

Herman stood up, holding his daughter tightly, then offered his chair to her.

Denise sat down, tearfully turning to the others. "How are they? How's my sister?"

Dr. Williams dreaded this part of his job, but gathered his courage, saying, "As you know, there was a car accident involving your family members. I worked on Savannah in the ER before she was moved into surgery. She has extensive injuries, and her condition is critical, but we won't know the full extent until she's out of the OR." The doctor continued, "I wish I had better news regarding the others."

The hair on the back of Denise's neck rose.

Jennifer reached over to hold her mother's hand for comfort.

Herman silently prayed for a miracle.

The doctor continued, "But their injuries were just too severe. They didn't survive the accident."

"No!" Denise shouted in disbelief, but the doctor's face told her it was true. She wept, resting her face in her hands.

Carol and Jennifer stared at each other with shock as tears of grief welled up in their eyes, filling until the dam broke and they began crying in earnest, falling into each others arms for support.

Herman stood there with a stoic face as memories flashed through his mind. He remembered celebrating his 60th birthday at the couple's beach house, and how the grandkids had hugged him after he blew out all the candles on his cake. He remembered walking Savannah down the aisle on her wedding day, and how proud Steve had looked waiting for her at the altar. Herman thought, *I've spent a lifetime preparing my daughter to grow up and have a family of her own, and now it's all been taken away.* His emotions vacillated between overwhelming anger and grief. He needed to sit down, but there were no available chairs.

Since there was nothing more Dr. Williams could do for this grieving family, he stood up, putting his hand on the door knob. He hesitated, then turned to face them one last time. "Please accept my condolences. Someone will be in here shortly to answer all of your questions. Again, I'm very sorry."

It was a tearful few minutes before the door opened again.

A woman entered with a police officer.

The woman, who had a hospital ID badge pinned to her suit, said, "First, let me extend my deepest sympathies for your loss. I am so sorry. I know this is a very traumatic time for you." She continued, "My name's Mrs. Miller, and I'm a grief counselor here at Duplin Hospital. And this is Officer Nolan. He was on duty at the accident scene. He can answer any questions you might have. But remember, even after tonight, I'm here to help you through this. I can assist with arrangements, phone calls and any other concerns you might have."

Herman weakly asked, "What happened?"

Mrs. Miller responded, "Officer Nolan, I believe you can best answer that question." She motioned for him to take the lead.

Officer Nolan made a dramatic show of pulling a notebook out of his front pocket, flipping it open, thumbing through the pages. The walkie-talkie attached to his belt crackled so he shut it off. He found the page he was looking for, then carefully withdrew the pen attached to the side, using it to mark something on the page.

Mrs. Miller unconsciously looked at the clock.

Denise grabbed a tissue from the box sitting on the desk, blowing her nose.

Officer Nolan finally spoke, "Keep in mind this is preliminary information. A formal report will be given to you after a full and thorough investigation." He then recited from his notes, "According to the truck driver behind the Watson family, they were traveling northwest on Highway 50 when they collided head-on with another vehicle."

Jennifer and Carol cried harder.

Herman's knees threatened to buckle.

A mixture of grief, shock and disbelief overcame Denise.

"After the collision, both vehicles rested in the middle of the highway. Unfortunately, the truck driver couldn't stop in time, stating 'the slick roads made it impossible.' His semi-truck hit the rear end of the Watson vehicle and propelled it into a guard rail."

Mrs. Miller felt the description was too graphic and loudly cleared her throat, trying to capture the officer's attention, but he didn't seem to notice and kept talking, "From there, their vehicle ricocheted and rolled, landing upright on the far side of the highway."

The entire family wept uncontrollably, except for Herman whose heart tightened as he tried to contain his emotions.

Officer Nolan snapped the notebook shut. "I want you to know that they died instantly—there was no pain or suffering." He paused, then said, "I am sorry to bring this up, but there is also the matter of identifying the deceased who are being held at the morgue. Because of the police investigation, there will be mandatory autopsies. Mrs. Miller can help with the arrangements—"

The officer stopped talking when Herman slid down the wall clutching his chest.

"Dad!" Denise shouted, jumping out of her chair. "Oh, my God! Somebody help him!" She knelt, clasping her father's hand, telling him, "You're going to be okay."

Mrs. Miller rushed to the door, flinging it open, shouting down the corridor, "Code Blue!"

Denise and Carol sat in a waiting room wondering if Herman would survive his surgery. The clock on the wall indicated it had been nearly six hours since his heart attack. Denise dabbed her red-rimmed tired eyes. Carol numbly stared at the row of empty chairs in front of them. This situation was too much to bear on top of the loss of the children and Steve. Not to mention Savannah's precarious condition. Even if she made it through the worst, she would still have to face a lifetime without her family. It was going to take all of their support to help her through this tragedy.

A surgeon wearing scrubs came out to speak with them. He removed the cap covering his salt-and-pepper hair out of respect, but his far-away look made it obvious that his mind was still inside the operating room. He asked the women, "Are you Herman Gomez's family?"

Denise nodded, saying, "I'm his daughter," then stood up to hear the news.

Carol struggled to her feet as well.

"I'm Doctor Randall. First, let me say, he's pulled through."

Denise let out a big sigh of relief.

"But we found significant blockages in three of his arteries, which mandated the need for bypass surgery. Once inside, we found damage to the heart, but it wasn't as bad as it could have been. He was damn lucky to be in a hospital when this happened."

"So he'll be fine?"

"He's stable, which is a good sign. He should wake up

within 12 to 16 hours, and once he does, we can better formulate a prognosis."

"What can you tell us about Savannah Watson's condition?" Denise asked.

"I'm not familiar with that case. I'm sure her doctors will let you know."

"Of course. Thank you for everything."

"You're very welcome." The surgeon strode away with an air of confidence acquired from decades of saving lives.

CHAPTER 4

The Aftermath

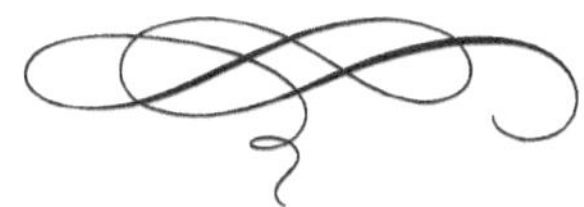

SAVANNAH LAY UNCONSCIOUS IN the Critical Care Unit. Her forehead was bandaged. Bruises covered her face and neck. Her legs were set in casts suspended by pulleys, weights and counterweights to keep them properly positioned. An assortment of bags and tubes dripped fluids into her IV lines. Numerous monitors blinked beside her bed.

Down the hall, Mrs. Miller and Dr. Johnson, the doctor on duty, sat in a small consulting room with Denise, who was making the medical decisions for her sister. Carol was there to offer moral support.

Dr. Johnson spoke first, "I know this is a very difficult time for you, but we need to discuss Savannah's condition. Right now, we have her heavily medicated to alleviate the pain. We also have her sedated, because if she were to regain consciousness, the news of her family might be more than she could bear. In addition, she sustained a traumatic head injury, which has led to swelling in her brain. Because of these factors, we are recommending that you allow us to put her into a medically induced coma."

Denise said, "That sounds serious."

"It is. But it would prevent additional brain swelling, as well as allow her time to stabilize. It will also prevent her from finding out about her family too soon. The news could definitely set her back. But before you decide, you should know that an induced coma means she will be hooked to a ventilator. Do you have any questions?"

Carol cleared her throat. "If I might ask, how long... how many days would she be in a coma?"

"Well, we'd make that decision based on her progress. When the swelling starts to recede that would be a positive indicator."

Denise asked in a trembling voice, "If Savannah's going to be unconscious for days, maybe weeks, how do we proceed with the funerals?"

Mrs. Miller answered this time, "As soon as the death certificates are issued, you can proceed."

"I guess what I'm really asking is, 'When will Savannah be able to attend?'"

"Doctor?" Mrs. Miller deferred to his judgment.

He cleared his throat, uncomfortable at giving bad news. "It could be a month before she's ready to leave the hospital, and even then she most likely would be transferred to a rehabilitation center. I know you want closure for her, but it's unrealistic to think she could attend funerals any time soon. If you feel it's really important for her to be there, you could request that they freeze the bodies."

Denise shuddered at the thought of her beloved niece and nephew lying frozen in storage.

Mrs. Miller mentioned in a hushed tone to the women, "I know this is unpleasant, but have you decided who will identify the bodies yet?"

Carol looked at Denise, who shook her head.

Mrs. Miller continued, "That needs to be done in order for the death certificates to be issued. I realize this is an unpleasant—" She paused, noticing that Denise was starting to breathe rapidly. "If none of you are up to it, perhaps you have a relative, such as an uncle or cousin, who can do it."

"Ron, my daughter's husband, might be able to," Carol suggested. "I think he has some medical training." She noticed Denise's distress, and reached over to pat her hand, asking, "Would that be all right with you?"

Denise pulled her hand away, placing it over her chest. Her breathing intensified.

"Are you okay?" Carol asked.

Dr. Johnson got up to evaluate Denise, taking the woman's wrist in his hand, checking her pulse. "See if you can slow down your breathing," he instructed. "Otherwise, you'll hyperventilate. Just stay calm. Take deep slow breaths."

Denise tried to control her breathing, but her heart beat faster and faster. She declared, "I think I'm having a heart attack!"

Carol frantically shouted, "Dear God! Do something!"

Dr. Johnson highly doubted the 35-year-old woman was having a heart attack, but he needed to follow protocol. "Stay calm. I'll get help." He opened the door, shouting at the nurse's station, "Code Blue!"

CHAPTER 5
The Morgue

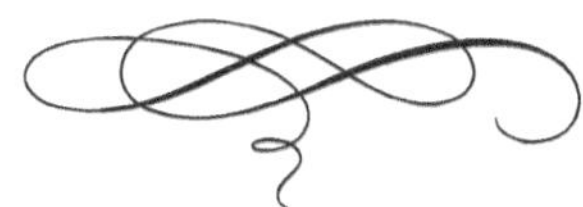

RON AND JENNIFER PULLED up in front of the Duplin County Morgue. Its brick facade and colonial-style windows resembled those of a funeral home. North Carolina's blazing sun beat down on the pair as they trudged across the hot pavement. The couple entered the lobby, grateful for the cool air.

They went up to the receptionist, who was sitting behind a glass partition, which she slid open, saying to them, "Welcome. Are you Ronald Smith?"

"I am," he answered.

"You're going to need to fill out the form." The receptionist pointed to the clipboard lying on the counter. "I'll also need to make a copy of your driver's license."

After doing as instructed, Ron sat next to his wife to

wait. His legs nervously shook.

A man's voice called out, "Ronald Smith?"

Fear and dread welled inside Ron when he looked up at the medical examiner dressed in a white lab coat standing at the end of the lobby, holding the wide metal door open with his shoulder. Ron got up. The knot in his stomach tightened with each footstep as he crossed the floor.

The medical examiner introduced himself, "I'm Doctor Forst. Sorry for your loss. Follow me, please."

They didn't walk far, stopping at the second door on the right-hand side. They entered a small dimly lit room. Two chairs were tucked under the countertop that held a viewing monitor.

The medical examiner explained, "Our cameras will provide images of your loved ones, unless you prefer to see the bodies in person."

Ron shook his head.

"I didn't think so. Most don't. Please have a seat," Dr. Forst pulled out a chair for the man. "When you're ready, we'll put the first image on the screen."

Ron sat in front of the monitor, feeling his heart pound in his chest. He wiped the sweat from his brow, then said, "Ready."

Dr. Forst hit the speaker button on the wall, instructing the technician in the morgue to present the first image.

On the monitor, Steve's pale and bruised face appeared. His jaw was slack.

Ron turned away. "That's him. Steve Watson." The sight caused his breathing to increase. He panicked, saying, "Oh, God. I don't think I can do this."

"Just take a moment. You'll get through this," Dr. Forst replied with a professional demeanor.

Ron thought to himself, *Why prolong the agony?* "Okay, I'm ready."

The medical examiner hit the speaker button again. "Next image, please."

The camera displayed Justin's face. There were no visible injuries.

"He looks like an angel," Ron sadly commented.

"Can you identify him?"

"Yes, that's Justin Watson."

"Just a moment while the technician sets up the camera. We just have the two."

A minute passed. A man's voice came over the speaker, "Ready."

Dr. Forst said, "Okay, here's the last one."

The screen showed Emily's face covered with cuts and bruises.

Ron confirmed, "That's Emily Watson."

CHAPTER 6

The Appearance

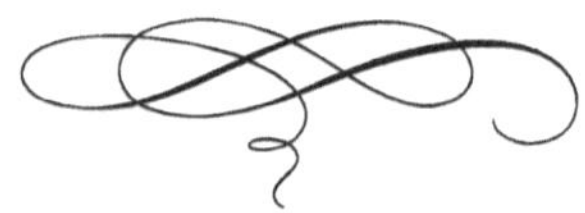

SEAGULLS SHRIEKED AND FLEW erratically as they searched for scraps on the beach.

Savannah sat on the wooden staircase that led from the deck to the sand below, acting as a bridge over the sawtoothed grass and sea oats that grew on the dunes. She leaned against the balusters, hugging the edge of a step with her bare toes while watching the beachgoers wade in the waves, which were a little too rough for her liking, but just right for the adventurous teenagers challenging the surf with their boogie boards.

The warmth of the sun was lulling her to sleep. Not a difficult task, because, for two nights in a row, she had the same disturbing dream, and the lack of sleep was taking its toll on her. Savannah closed her eyes, listening to the waves roll over the shore. The ocean breeze caressed her skin and fluttered her hair. She embraced the perfection of the moment.

Until she felt the presence of someone near her.

Savannah instinctively opened her eyes, stunned to see the gauzy spirit of a man standing before her, resting his hand on the rail. His semi-transparent form quickly solidified. The ocean that had glistened through his transparent body was now hidden behind his blue robe tied with a red sash, flapping in the light wind. He had long brown hair that hung over his shoulders and a beard. His gentle face held loving eyes that looked directly at her. And, despite the sun's glare, she noticed a golden aura outlining his body.

The man greeted her, "Hello, Savannah."

She felt the overpowering love pouring out of him. A knowing entered Savannah's heart. There was no doubt in her mind who he was. She called out, "Jesus!" pleased by his sudden and unexpected arrival—amazed at how natural it felt to see him in the flesh.

"Do you mind if I sit with you?" Jesus Christ asked.

"Not at all! Please do!"

She gestured with her hand, indicating that he was more than welcome to sit beside her, which he did.

Jesus said, "You were thinking that this moment is

perfect. What does perfection mean to you?"

Savannah hesitated before answering him, afraid of saying the wrong thing, but his warm smile encouraged her. "Well, perfection means...no worries, no fears, no problems to solve."

Jesus knew she hadn't completed her thoughts and patiently waited for her to continue.

"Well...that's not exactly how I would define it. Perfection means no possibility of anything going wrong. Ever."

Jesus pointed at a seagull flying over the beach. "You see that bird?"

Savannah nodded.

"It is perfect. You see him?" He pointed to a man, sitting in a beach chair, who was red as a lobster and sported a beer belly that hung over his swim trunks. "He is perfect."

She raised her eyebrows skeptically. "You must be talking about our spiritual selves and not our physical selves."

"You think there is a physical self?"

"Yes, of course."

"Do you think I see a physical world?" he inquired.

Savannah gave his question some thought, then replied, "Yes, but I assume you see both the physical and spiritual worlds at the same time. The best of both worlds."

"Tell me. What is the best of this world?"

"Um...well...there's the love for my family, and theirs for me—and my friends, of course."

"Anything else?"

"Um...I guess the rest is gravy. You know...the icing on the cake."

"I am familiar with your slang," Jesus responded kindly.

She blushed at her condescending remark. "Of course, I'm sorry."

"There's nothing to be sorry for."

They stopped talking and watched two teenagers strolling on the beach, licking their ice cream.

Jesus asked, "If you were to lose your friends and family, what would be the best of this world then?"

Before Savannah could answer, her husband opened and closed the sliding glass door while balancing a metal platter of raw hamburgers in his other hand. He walked toward the grill, but came to a standstill when he saw a man sitting next to his wife.

Savannah called out, "Steve! You will never guess who's here! It's Jesus!"

The Son of God stood up, his robe waving in the breeze. His aura shimmered.

The platter that Steve held slowly tipped forward. The hamburgers slid off, plopping onto the wooden boards. Then the platter fell out of his hands, clanging onto the deck, spinning round and round, finally landing at the edge of the stairs near Jesus.

Steve fainted, falling flat on his back.

"Oh, my God!" Savannah shouted as she jumped up, but before rushing to her husband's side, she turned toward Jesus, saying, "Sorry." Then she moved ahead, kneeling beside Steve, feeling the back of his head to make sure he hadn't hurt himself.

Jesus said to her, "Let me help you get him inside."

He scooped Steve into his arms while Savannah opened the glass door. Jesus carried the unconscious man into the living room, gently laying him on the sofa. Savannah put a pillow under her husband's head.

The kids had heard their mother's outburst and clambered out of their bedrooms, rushing down the stairs to see what was going on.

"Why's Dad on the couch?" asked 12-year-old Justin, rightly concerned.

"Mom, is Dad all right?" the eldest of the two, 15-year-old Emily, demanded to know, then she stared at her father making her own assessment, absentmindedly holding her phone.

"He just fainted—that's all," Savannah answered, trying to ease her children's fears.

At the same time, the kids noticed the stranger standing beside their mother. A stranger who looked remarkably like Jesus Christ. Justin and Emily looked at each other, inquisitively raising their eyebrows.

Justin brought up the elephant in the room, "Mom, who's this?"

Jesus smiled as he walked over to the young man, holding out his hand. "Hello, Justin. It's good to meet you. My name is Jesus."

Justin vigorously returned the handshake, relishing the moment. "This is so cool!"

Emily wasn't so sure about the situation and stood back.

Jesus understood her hesitation and didn't approach her. Instead, he simply said, "Hello, Emily. It's nice to meet you."

She wondered how he knew her name, but decided that her mother had already told him. Her thoughts wandered back to her father, who remained unconscious. "Are you sure he's okay?" Emily leaned over, poking his cheek.

Her action prodded Steve awake. He opened his eyes, blurting, "What happened?"

Justin squealed with delight, "Dad! You're all right!"

Steve looked at his son, but then noticed Jesus standing beside him. The sight caused the father to faint a second time.

"Crap! He's out again," Justin said.

"Justin, don't use that word! Especially in front of Jesus," Savannah scolded him.

Unfazed, her son challenged Jesus, "So if you're the real deal, why don't you just make my dad stop fainting?"

"When he is ready, he will stop. Right now, the situation is a bit much for him to take in."

"He'll be all right though. Right?"

"Yes. He'll be fine."

Justin was relieved enough to suggest, "How about a game of Crazy Eights until he wakes up?"

Emily scoffed, "Not again! I'm sick of that game."

While the kids bickered, Savannah bent over to gently shake her husband by his shoulder. When he came around, she whispered, "Why don't you talk with Jesus? It's the chance of a lifetime."

Steve peered over his wife's shoulder at the man who claimed to be the Son of God, and then back at her, muttering, "He's a fake."

"Then why do you keep fainting?" Savannah pointed out.

Refusing to be cornered, Steve asked, "If he's really Jesus, why would he visit us?"

"Don't you think he visits everyone?"

"No. Not if they don't believe in him."

"Well, I think he does. Especially those who don't believe in him."

Jesus approached the couple.

Savannah stepped away to give them privacy.

"What are you afraid of?" Jesus asked Steve.

The man's face paled.

Jesus said what was on the man's mind, "You think I'm an impostor."

Steve nodded.

"What would prove to you that I am the embodiment of Christ?"

Not knowing what the word "embodiment" meant in this context, Steve couldn't answer him.

Jesus explained, "In this situation, embodiment means the physical manifestation of Christ."

Steve was not a religious man, and knew very little of the Bible or its teachings, so even the word "Christ" was ambiguous in his mind.

Again, Jesus explained, "Christ is the Son of God. The expression of His love."

Steve asked, "Who is God?"

"God is love. Always has been and always will be."

The kids, who were eavesdropping, came closer.

Justin interjected, "If God is love and he made us, then we are love. Right?"

"Yes. Very good, Justin."

Emily pointed out, "Well, Justin doesn't always act loving. This morning, he pulled my hair when I wouldn't let him change the TV channel."

Jesus found her comment humorous, saying to her, "On the shows that you watch, sometimes the actors are hateful, jealous and even violent. Why would anyone watch bad things on the television when they avoid them in their everyday life?"

Emily smugly answered, "Everyone knows the shows aren't real."

Jesus gazed into her big brown eyes, asking her, "Do you believe heaven is real?"

She didn't hesitate to answer, "No. I don't believe in God or heaven."

"But you believe I am Jesus?"

"Yeah...you're standing right in front of me." She sighed at the obvious answer.

"So do you need to see something for it to be real? For instance, have you ever seen love? Or do you merely see the acts that express love?"

"You're trying to trick me," Emily accused him.

He smiled. "Not at all. My point is, you can't see what is real here on earth—only reflections of the truth."

Then Jesus disappeared from their sight.

CHAPTER 7

Beach Cookout

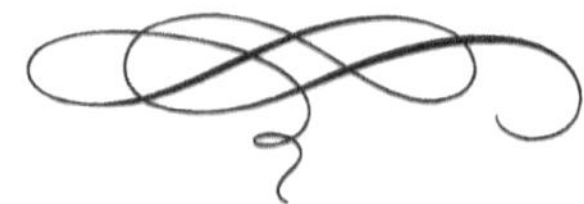

NIGHT HAD COME AND Steve was setting up a portable gas-powered fire pot, in lieu of a traditional bonfire, to adhere to the local ordinances prohibiting open fires on the beach. Finished with that task, he headed back to the house to load the ice chest with soft drinks.

Justin stood over the fire pot, loudly saying, "Higher! Higher!" while swirling his arms, pretending to be a magician creating flames out of thin air.

His mother said to him, "Honey, please go help your dad carry stuff down."

Justin sprinted across the sand to catch up with his father.

With everyone gone, Savannah sat watching the flames curl past the steel grate. The recurring dream of the car accident was bothering her again.

Jesus appeared, standing tall on the sand, the flames highlighting his form.

Savannah was pleasantly surprised by his unexpected arrival. "Hello! It's good to see you again."

"Hello, Savannah. Do you mind if I sit with you?"

"Not at all." She scooted over on the blanket to make room for him.

He sat down, adjusting his robe over his legs.

Savannah took this opportunity to ask for his help. "I had that same dream again last night. Can you make it stop?"

Jesus posed his own question to her, "Have you ever tried to walk with a glass of water while thinking, 'Don't spill it?' What happens?"

"You spill it."

"Why do you suppose that is?"

She sighed. "I suppose it's because you're thinking about it too much, but my dream is different. It comes of its own accord—"

Their conversation was interrupted when Justin called out, "Jesus!" then ran over, hugging him. When the young man stepped back, he exclaimed, "I can't wait to see how you roast marshmallows!" He shouted at his sister, who was headed toward them, "Hurry up and bring the stuff!"

Emily scowled. She was irritated that Justin hadn't helped carry the bags and boxes of snacks that she held.

Steve trailed behind his daughter, dragging the ice chest over the sand.

Savannah warned her husband, "Honey, stay away from the fire pot. I don't want you to faint and burn yourself."

He looked over at her, noticing Jesus sitting there. Steve set the ice chest down, put his hands on his waist, and then accusingly said to the Son of God, "I don't believe you're really Jesus, and I am tired of you scamming my family. So leave."

Immediately, Jesus disappeared from the man's sight, causing Steve to faint once more. The sand softened his fall.

"Not again." Emily sighed.

Savannah looked at Jesus. "Why did he faint? He's seen you before."

"He believes I disappeared."

Justin shrugged his shoulders, then handed Jesus a stick and a marshmallow.

Savannah got up, walking over to Steve. She bent down, shaking him. "Wake up!"

Steve opened his eyes. "Is he gone?"

"No, he's not gone. You just can't see him. There's a

difference," she said, annoyed by his resistance.

It was then that Steve noticed the stick with a marshmallow stuck to its tip floating over the fire. "I know you're still here!" he called out.

Jesus reappeared, pulling his stick out of the fire to examine the roasted marshmallow. "I believe it's ready." After roasting several more, he walked over and sat in the sand next to Steve, who had stayed where he fell, laying on his back and gazing at the stars.

Without moving, Steve asked Jesus, "What's it like to travel to the stars?"

"Everything contains God's power so technically visiting a star is no different than visiting you."

"Can you talk with stars?"

"I would describe it more as communicating than talking."

"Why am I so afraid of you?"

"The real question is, 'Why are you afraid of knowing who *you* really are?'"

As if on cue, a shooting star streaked across the sapphire sky.

Steve turned his head toward Jesus, then, in a feeble attempt to change the subject, he asked, "What did that shooting star have to say?"

"Like all things, it was expressing love."

"And now that it's gone?"

"I guess you could ask me the same question, since I appeared to have died on the cross. You see—the physical form is not relevant. Not when your spirit lives forever."

"How about dolphins? Can you talk with dolphins?"

Jesus smiled, glad that the man had a sense of humor about the subject, then he turned toward the fire, watching the kids and Savannah enjoy the evening. "I think I'll roast another marshmallow," he commented, getting to his feet to join the others.

Steve quipped, "Isn't that marshmallow torture?" as he stood up to follow Jesus, grabbing his own stick, stabbing it into a marshmallow, bellowing, "I am Steven the Terrible! Ruler of no one and a marshmallow killer!" He held the stick high and thrust his chest toward the sky.

The group's silhouette was outlined by the fire that burned in the night. The waves lapped against the shore. At the top of the dunes stood their house, its lights glowing through the windows, acting as a beacon to welcome them home when they were ready to return.

CHAPTER 8

Recoveries

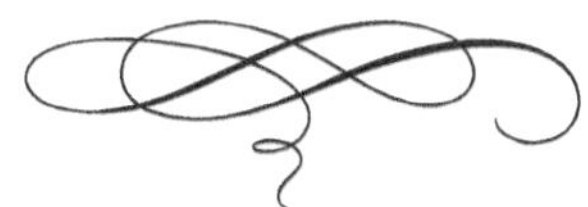

AT THE EARLIEST VISITING hour, Carol exited an elevator, traveling down a hospital corridor, stepping into a room where Denise lay in a bed reading a celebrity magazine. Her eye makeup was still smudged and her hair was a mess.

"How are you feeling today?" Carol inquired, concerned about the younger woman's unsightly appearance.

Denise grinned, slurring her words, "Great! I don't know what they put me on, but it's working."

"You're drugged!"

"Am I?"

Carol tersely said, "Well, it turns out you didn't have a heart attack. It was just an anxiety attack so you'll be discharged—"

"Just an anxiety attack! My blood pressure was sky high! I could have had a stroke!" Denise exclaimed too loudly.

Ignoring the dramatic outburst, Carol told her, "I'm going to stop by to see your dad before seeing Savannah. I'll let you know if the doctors have anything new to say."

In the elevator, Carol leaned against the wall fighting back the tears as she headed to the third floor.

The metal door slid open.

She walked down the hallway toward Herman's room.

Carol was shocked when she saw him. The color was gone from his sunken face. His wrinkles had deepened. She politely pretended not to notice. "Hello, there."

"Hi," Herman answered, raising the remote in his hand, muting the television.

"I hope you're feeling better."

"Been better. Should be out of here tomorrow, though."

"Tomorrow? Are you sure? Seems a little soon."

"I'm leaving tomorrow—no matter what. They're just keeping me here to make more money. It's always about the money," he growled.

"Well, in your case, it was pretty serious. Although it was a blessing it happened while you were in the hospital."

He ignored her comment, instead asking, "Where's Denise?"

"Oh...well...umm," Carol stammered. "You see...there was a slight problem yesterday."

Herman grew concerned, raising his head.

She wasn't quite sure how to break the bad news to him. She clutched her purse a little tighter. "You see... um...Denise and I were talking with the doctor about Savannah, and, well, Denise got very upset, because we were talking about, you know, difficult stuff." Then as quickly as possible Carol told him, "Anyway, after getting upset, Denise had an anxiety attack and had to be hospitalized, but she's all right, and should be out today."

Herman's eyes bulged and his face turned red with anger. "This place will kill us all before we get out of here! They're incompetent! Can't touch anything without breaking it."

Carol braced herself against his ranting, saying nothing to avoid fueling his fire. Her approach seemed to work.

He calmed down, taking a deep breath, fidgeting with his bedding. "So how is Savannah doing?"

"She's still unconscious, but stable." Carol purposely didn't use the word "coma" for fear it would set Herman off again, especially if he knew the doctors had induced it.

His voice quivered as he asked, "Is she going to be all right?"

Carol gently answered, "I have faith that she will."

Later that day, Denise was handed her discharge papers. After tidying herself up and changing into her street clothes, she went up to the Critical Care Unit. The corridors were quiet, and the patients were even quieter.

She entered her sister's room. The sight of Savannah's injuries was sobering as Denise watched the breathing tube pump air into her lungs. Leaning over, she stroked Savannah's hair, whispering, "It's going to be all right. No matter what, sis, remember it's going to be all right."

CHAPTER 9
The Grocery Store

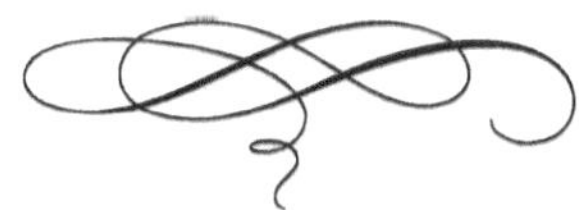

WHILE THE KIDS AND Steve were playing at the beach, Savannah and Jesus were at the grocery store strolling through the produce department, which was filled with bright colors and fresh smells.

"Look, avocados are on sale," Savannah mentioned. She tested several for ripeness, then put one in the cart. Under her breath, she asked, "Can people hear me talking to you?"

Jesus replied, "Of course, they can. However, they can't see or hear me. If you prefer, we can speak telepathically."

Savannah thought, *That would be best*, then she picked up a bag of grapes, commenting, *That dream keeps bothering me. It comes almost every night, and it seems so real, progressing like a morbid soap opera. Between you and the dream, I'm starting to feel like I'm losing my mind.*

Why does the dream bother you so much?

Because I fear it's a premonition.

Do you think it's possible to foresee the future?

Yes.

And who is showing it to you?

God?

Jesus responded, *You are very close. The Voice for God does speak to you, and sometimes warns you of impending events, which would prevent you from fulfilling your destiny, allowing you to sidestep them. However, this dream doesn't feel like Divine intervention to you, does it?*

No. It feels more like an unstoppable omen.

They walked out of the produce department and into the next aisle.

Savannah asked Jesus, *So is it an omen or Divine intervention? Or just a dream?*

How do you know you're awake now?

She tossed a bag of cookies into the cart and sighed. *Your riddles aren't helping me. I'm so upset about this dream I can't sleep at night.*

They strolled down the next aisle where she selected a bottle of ketchup.

Jesus pointed to jars of green olives, saying, *I believe*

these are on your list.

Thanks. Savannah crossed it off the slim piece of paper in her hand. *I'm kind of dreading the meat department. Are you opposed to killing animals for food?*

Do you think a spirit can be a body?

I think a spirit can reside in a body, she replied.

How does it reside in a body?

Savannah answered, *You know, in it. Not really part of it, just in it.*

Then what is the purpose of the body?

Well, we can't do much without it.

Do you think a spirit can communicate without a body?

You mean like a ghost?

A woman shopper interrupted their silent conversation, asking, "Can I get in here?" She pointed at the brand of bread she wanted.

"Sorry, I'll move out of your way," Savannah apologized as she absentmindedly grabbed a loaf, throwing it in the cart, continuing down the aisle.

Jesus rephrased his question, *Do you think spiritual beings can communicate with people here on earth?*

Well, you are, so obviously it's possible, but not very common.

So one might say that the body limits communication.

Savannah stopped at the end of the aisle, looking at

the meat section in front of them. *Speaking of bodies—is it okay if we eat meat? I don't want to offend you.*

There's nothing you could do that would offend me.

"Then I'm buying steaks!" Savannah blurted out loud.

A few shoppers glanced her way.

You're out of steak sauce, Jesus mentioned.

After paying for the groceries, Savannah and Jesus walked across the hot parking lot to her SUV, putting the groceries in the cargo area, then got in. Savannah started the engine, immediately flipping on the air to cool down the interior.

She drove out of the lot, turning onto the main street, heading back to Topsail Island. With Jesus sitting beside her, she cruised past the gaudy souvenir shops where tourists exited with their newly purchased beach towels, boogie boards, t-shirts, hats and protective body suits—anticipating a fun day at the beach.

Savannah came to a halt at the red light. While waiting, she noticed white flashes darting above her vehicle. She leaned forward, peering up through the windshield.

Hundreds of doves were flying in a spiral that reached high into the sky—a captivating sight for the people stopped at the light and those driving through the intersection.

"That's not normal, is it?" she asked.

Jesus just smiled at her.

The car behind her honked. The traffic light had turned green. Savannah stepped on the gas.

Some of the doves flew ahead of them like guardian angels preparing the way while the remaining congregation closely followed the SUV as it crossed over the bridge. The houses, nestled along the marsh below, served as a scenic backdrop.

"Can everyone see them?" she asked Jesus, referring to the birds.

"Yes."

She unconsciously scooted down in her seat as if a driverless car would be less noticeable.

After Savannah finished putting away the groceries, the phone rang. She answered it, "Hello?"

"Hello to you!" her sister replied cheerfully. Denise was sitting on the sofa with her feet propped on the coffee table, waiting for the polish on her toenails to dry. "I was wondering if I could join you for dinner and spend the night? I'd like to catch some rays in the morning."

"Sure. We're eating at six so come early."

"I'll be there."

"See 'ya!"

After hanging up the phone, Savannah glanced at Jesus, who was sitting at the kitchen table. She wondered if she should tell Denise about the Son of God coming into their lives—literally.

Jesus understood her concern. "Would you like to walk along the beach with me? We can talk about it."

"Sure, just let me change first."

Ten minutes later, they strolled along the shoreline. Savannah wore cut-off jeans with a red-striped tank top and a straw hat that tied under her chin. Jesus' robe fluttered in the ocean breeze. The Watson's beach house could be seen behind them with an unusual number of doves roosting on the rooftop and deck. The salty haze added a mystical element to the setting.

Sunbathers lay on multi-colored towels. Swimmers bobbed in the waves. Young marines, who were taking a little R&R from the Camp Lejeune base, played touch football.

A three-year-old boy scooped sand into his bucket. He looked up at Savannah and Jesus, smiling at them.

Jesus leaned down, patting the boy's small head before moving on.

"Why did you decide to show yourself to me and my family?" Savannah asked.

"You have it backwards. You decided to see me."

"See, that concerns me, because you came at the same time that the dream started. Is something bad going to happen? Is that why you're here?" She waited anxiously for his response.

"People are often afraid when they 'see' God. What if I told you I am only here because you were ready to see me. Nothing more. Nothing less." He took a few more strides. "Why don't you ask me some of those questions that you always wanted answers to?"

Savannah liked that idea. "Okay. Why do bad things happen to good people?"

"First, let me clarify that people are neither good nor bad."

"Now, you're just trying to start an argument," she sputtered.

He smiled.

She blushed. "Okay, I don't really believe you'd start an argument. I'm just having a hard time believing there aren't bad people."

"Well, let's go through this logically. First, do you think God is a spirit or body?"

"A spirit."

"So if God made you in his image—wouldn't you also be a spirit?"

"I guess that makes sense, but where does the body come into this?"

"If you are a spirit, how can you be a body?"

"Because I have one," she said, lifting her arms, spinning around in a circle to demonstrate the proof of her physical form. "You can't deny I have a body."

He kindly regarded her playfulness, and, instead of disagreeing with her, he said, "When you no longer see yourself as separate from God, you will see yourself as you truly are—a perfect spirit."

"Is that how you see me, right now?"

"'See' wouldn't be the correct term. 'Know' would be more accurate. Although with your current belief in time and space, it's impossible for you to fully comprehend that you are a spirit in complete unison with God, even as we speak."

The waves washed over their feet.

Jesus completed his answer, "I know you as love—communicating perfectly with the Father and all of His Creation."

Savannah quietly asked, "Can you show me how the world looks through your eyes?"

The ocean, sky and sand dissolved into a golden light.

Rays of light extended from the Son of God's soul to the heavens.

Savannah felt the eternal love, ebbing and flowing with all of existence, pulsating through her.

Then it all stopped.

The golden light was once again cloaked by the physical form.

Savannah looked at the ocean's sandy water sluggishly lapping at the shore. "Why did it stop?"

"Because that was all you could accept. It's always your choice," Jesus answered. "Ready to head back?"

She turned around.

"Regarding 'bad things' happening," Jesus said, "It may be difficult for you to accept, but God doesn't do anything to you. This is your life. You manifest everything that happens to you."

"Okay, I have two problems with that statement. First, God created me so it would seem he creates everything that happens to me, and second, I'm just a person. I can't create all of this." Savannah stretched out her arms wide to represent the whole world.

Jesus replied, "Let's go back to what I said previously about you being a spirit. If you're a spirit, created in God's image, then you would have all of His power. And if you had all of that power, then you certainly could create this life and everything that happens to you in it." He added, "The real problem is you don't see yourself that way. You see yourself as an insignificant and limited woman—a victim to the whims of this world. It is only because you don't fully recognize yourself as God's Creation that you doubt what I am saying."

Savannah sighed. "I just can't get past not seeing myself as a body."

"Yet you also believe you are a spirit. You will remain conflicted as long as you try to reconcile being both flesh and spirit."

"Is it wrong to think of myself as a body?"

"You are free to think of yourself however you would like, for as long as you would like, but, eventually, you will see yourself as you really are. How long you wish to procrastinate is up to you."

They reached the bottom of the steps leading up to the beach house. Samson, the family's black Labrador, bounded over to greet them. He dropped a tennis ball at Savannah's feet, licking her legs, and then Jesus' hand. Since neither of them seemed interested in throwing the ball, he snatched it with his mouth, sprinting back toward the kids.

"Mom!" both Emily and Justin shouted as they ran up to her, kicking up sand, their cheeks and noses rosy from too much sun.

Justin looked up at the house, asking, "What's with all

the birds!?" He didn't wait for the answer. "That is so cool! I'm getting my phone!" He rushed up the deck stairs.

Steve came into view, carrying the towels and dragging the boogie boards by their cords. Savannah thought how handsome he looked—tan from the sun, and tired after a day of playing with their children.

Justin reached the top of the stairs, dashing across the deck toward the house, startling the doves from their roosts along the railing, eavestrough and rooftop. The birds fluttered overhead.

Steve exclaimed, "Holy crap! What's with all the birds? Are those seagulls? No, wait...those are doves."

"They just sort of appeared when we were coming back from the grocery store," Savannah explained.

"They followed you home!?"

She tilted her head toward Jesus, indicating that she felt the birds had followed him, not her.

"Wow!" Steve climbed the stairs to get a better look. The others stepped behind him.

At the top, Emily commented, "I feel like I'm at a bird sanctuary."

"I feel like I'm in a Hitchcock movie," Steve stated.

"A what?"

"Never mind."

Steve, Savannah and Emily ducked to avoid the birds.

Jesus calmly walked across the deck, knowing the doves meant them no harm.

After everyone was inside, Savannah and Jesus went into the kitchen while Steve and Emily remained near the sliding glass door, staring outside. The air was so white with doves that the ocean was barely visible beyond their flapping wings.

"This is getting really weird, Dad," Emily commented.

"It might get even weirder," he responded, not taking his eyes off the spectacle.

Justin stepped beside them, excitedly recording the doves with his phone.

Denise arrived at the beach house driving her Fiat convertible with the top down. Her dog, Blanca, a pampered Bichon Frise, was strapped into a raised dog seat, looking adorable with pink bows tied above her ears. Denise's tan glowed gorgeously against her coral blouse with capped sleeves and a low neckline. She checked her lipstick in the mirror, grabbed her suitcase-sized purse from the back seat, then unstrapped Blanca.

As she walked up the stairs carrying her dog, she noticed the large flock of doves perched on the roof, cooing. "What the heck is going on!?" she wondered out loud. Blanca squirmed with excitement, yelping.

Concerned that the dog might jump out of her arms, Denise quickly opened the door, rushing inside where she announced, "I'm here!"

The kids came running, yelling, "Aunt Denise!" After a quick hug, they took Blanca from her.

Samson cowered at the sight of the other dog, hiding behind Savannah, keeping an eye on the little princess of terror.

Savannah waited to see if her sister would notice Jesus standing beside her, but Denise simply walked over and hugged her. However, she did notice the throng of doves covering the deck.

Denise let go of Savannah. "What's with all the birds?"

Justin, who was petting Blanca on the floor, absentmindedly said, "They're here because Jesus is here."

"Honey, Jesus is everywhere."

He looked up. "Yeah, but he really is here."

"Really?" she scoffed. "Where is he?"

"Next to Mom."

Savannah smiled sheepishly and shrugged her shoulders, then nervously said, "Justin, we'll talk about it later. Okay?"

Denise sensed the tension so she changed the subject.

"Well, I'm going to put on my swimsuit and catch some rays before dinner." She headed up to the guest room to change.

Justin waited until his aunt was out of sight before asking his mother, "Aren't we going to tell her?" He continued rubbing Blanca's belly.

"I don't know."

"Why wouldn't we?"

"People tend to think you're crazy when you tell them you see Jesus."

Denise, who was listening at the top of the stairs, stifled a gasp, then quietly went to her room.

CHAPTER 10

Out of a Coma

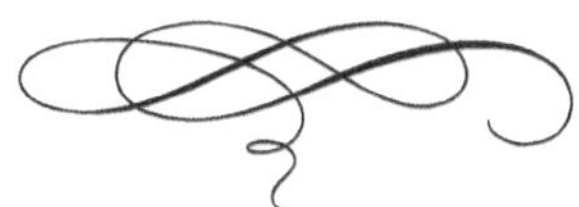

THE FIFTH DAY AFTER the accident, Savannah's doctor was ready to take her out of the induced coma. Denise, Carol and Jennifer waited nearby. Herman, who had been discharged that morning, sat in a hospital-furnished wheelchair.

Dr. Johnson stood over the unconscious patient with a nurse by his side. He explained, "After the tube is removed and the medicine drip is stopped, it will take several hours for Savannah to regain consciousness, and even then, I expect her to be extremely groggy. We're also starting her on pain medication so she'll be sleepy from that as well. I wouldn't expect much from her for a couple of days, maybe longer."

Carol asked, "Will there be any side effects? From the coma?"

"There can be. Sometimes a patient experiences vivid hallucinations—so just humor her if this happens. Once she's fully conscious, she'll realize they're not real. She may also be confused about where she is, or not remember the accident, which is normal for an accident victim with a head injury. Please don't offer her any information unless she asks. We're still concerned that the news of her family's deaths will set her back. People do better when they have something to live for. Any more questions?" Dr. Johnson asked as a courtesy, but he obviously was on a tight schedule.

"No, thank you, doctor," Carol said.

"Well, we're ready to start the procedure. To spare you, we're going to close the curtain while we do this."

The family waited in the room on the other side.

A minute later, the nurse opened the curtain. Without the tube, Savannah looked more like her old self. Now they just needed to wait for her to wake up.

On his way out, Dr. Johnson looked at Herman in the wheelchair, advising him, "You might be more comfortable sitting in the recliner while you wait. The nurse can help you."

"I can do it myself, thank you," he replied tersely.

"I'm sure you can," the doctor agreed, glancing at the wristband still attached to Herman's arm. "However, it would be wise to take it easy for the next few days. Let us help you, at least while you're here."

As soon as Dr. Johnson left the room, Herman complained, "See...this is what happens when you're down and out. People start treating you like an invalid. Next, they'll be feeding me with a spoon."

Denise rolled her eyes. She was used to her father's complaining.

Jennifer quelled her irritation over the man's rantings.

The nurse stepped forward, ready to assist Herman.

Hours later, Herman had fallen asleep in the recliner. Jennifer went home to take care of her family while Carol remained, sitting patiently in a chair next to Savannah's bedside, waiting for her to regain consciousness.

Denise had gone to the vending machine, and returned eating out of a bag of Cheetos and carrying a can of Pepsi.

Suddenly, Savannah woke up screaming.

Herman bolted upright, clutching his chest and stammering, "What!? What?"

Carol jumped up from her chair to comfort her daughter-in-law.

Denise rushed across the room. Bits of fluorescent-orange food flew through the air. Cola splashed over her clothes and the floor, but by the time she reached Savannah, her sister had closed her eyes, unconscious once more.

CHAPTER 11

Reoccurring Dream

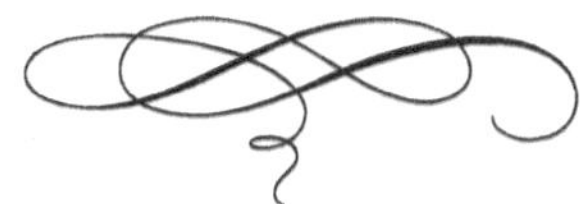

IN THE MIDDLE OF the night, Savannah screamed.

Steve woke up, frantically scanning the bedroom, expecting to find an intruder. It was only after Savannah stopped screaming that he realized she was having that dream again. He reached over to comfort her. "It's all right. It's all right."

She began crying.

"It was just a dream," he said, holding her tightly.

In the guest room, Denise had also been abruptly pulled out of sleep. Wanting to know what was wrong, she hustled to her sister's bedroom, wrapping a robe around herself along the way. Blanca scurried beside her.

Denise knocked. When there was no answer, she gingerly opened the door, peering inside. She saw her sister lying in bed in Steve's arms. A sliver of moonlight streaked across Savannah's face, reflecting the tears running down her cheeks. "Is everything okay?"

Savannah, who was embarrassed to be seen this way, tried to compose herself, explaining, "I just had a bad dream. That's all."

Her sister sensed something more was going on, but she also felt she was intruding on Steve's territory. "Do you need anything? A glass of water, maybe?"

"No, thanks, I'm fine. Really. It was just a dream," Savannah assured her.

"Okay, I'll see you in the morning," Denise said, then gently shut the door.

She walked down the hall, but instead of going to her room, she went downstairs, planning to sit outside on the deck, hoping the ocean's sights and sounds would calm her nerves.

Unfortunately for Denise, she had forgotten about the multitude of doves. As soon as she and Blanca stepped outside, the dog went berserk—barking and racing around, rousing the sleeping birds, which burst into flight, white against the night, creating a snowstorm of feathers as they circled, cooing loudly, stirring the others on the roof, adding to the commotion.

Denise screeched, crouching and covering her head.

Meanwhile, Blanca was having a grand time leaping and nipping at the doves. The woman managed to catch the little dog mid-jump, carrying her back inside, closing the door before placing her on the floor.

Denise took a deep breath, regained her composure, then walked toward the stairs with feathers falling behind her. Blanca happily hopped up and down, trying to catch each one as it fluttered to the carpet.

Sunday breakfast was an elaborate affair at the Watson household. Savannah was cooking bacon, pancakes, fried potatoes, grits and scrambled eggs.

The kids were watching the television in the living room.

Steve, who had just finished taking a shower, was getting dressed.

Samson lay near the oven keeping a wary eye on Blanca, who sat obediently at her mistress's feet under the dining table.

Denise asked, "So do you want to tell me about the dream?"

Savannah kept stirring the scrambled eggs. "No, not really,"

"Are you okay?"

"Yes, I'm fine."

"If it's something else, you can tell me. I am your sister."

"No, really. It was just the dream."

"Well, it must have been a nightmare to make you scream like that."

"It was."

Denise paused, then insisted, "Just tell me. I have to know."

"Fine, if you must know, I've had the same dream every night for almost a week. There's a car accident, and the kids and Steve are killed."

"Oh, no!"

"The worst part is—" Savannah stopped talking for a moment to slide the eggs from the frying pan onto a plate. "The worst part is, it seems so real. Every detail is there. The ambulances...the hospital...identifying the bodies. I feel scared and guilty at the same time."

"I'm so sorry," Denise said sympathetically.

Savannah set the plate of eggs on the table next to the pancakes. "Breakfast is ready!" she shouted.

The kids rushed to the table.

Steve came down the stairs and took his seat. He began reading out loud from his tablet, "Says this afternoon will be sunny, but a bit cooler than normal."

Savannah took her place at the table, pleased by

what she saw before her. The food looked delicious. Her husband, kids and sister hungrily prepared their own plates. Savannah was grateful for the abundance of love that surrounded her, yet she also was afraid of losing it. The black train haunted her memory. She could hear its metal wheels pounding on the tracks, faster and faster. The train whistle shrieked like a hawk ready to strike—growing louder and louder until it hurt her ears, causing her to clutch her head.

Her family stopped putting food on their plates.

Savannah felt their eyes on her. The sound of the train faded. She put her hands down, saying, "I'm all right... just tired that's all." She used her fork to grab a pancake, throwing it on her plate, trying to act as if nothing was wrong.

Everyone slowly started eating, but Denise kept glancing at her sister wondering if she should say or do something.

After breakfast, Steve and the kids cleared the table, giving Savannah and Denise a chance to spend some time together.

The women went to the beach where they sat on a blanket near the grass-covered dunes.

Denise had been dying to ask Savannah about the

"Jesus subject" ever since she had eavesdropped the evening before. "So...what did Justin mean about Jesus being here? Did you start going to church?"

Savannah tried to deflect the conversation. "Since when do you find our lives interesting? Usually, you have something more exciting to talk about. Like a new boyfriend."

Denise almost took the bait, replying, "Yeah, there is someone I've got my eye on..." then she remembered her original question, "but, right now, I want to know what Justin meant when he said, 'Jesus is here.' That's not something you hear everyday."

Savannah stared at the ocean wondering how it would affect their relationship if she told her sister the truth. *Will she think I'm crazy?* she wondered.

Denise prodded her. "If you can't tell your sister, who can you tell?"

Savannah decided to trust her. "A few days ago, I was sitting on the deck and Jesus appeared."

"What? Are you serious?"

"Yes. Very. He looked like a real man, except I could feel the love pouring out of him, and he had this golden aura around him. And ever since he's been here, he's answered all sorts of questions. It's almost been like an intervention—like I'm at a crossroad of some sort. His presence is comforting, yet, at the same time, it scares me because I keep having this bad dream, and I can't help but wonder if he showed up because I'm about to experience a horrible tragedy. Maybe the dream's an omen."

"Did you ask him about the dream? What am I saying? Now I'm acting like Jesus is really visiting you."

"Oh, he is. The kids and Steve see him as well," said Savannah. "He was standing there when you arrived."

"Um...I hate to break it to you, but I didn't see him. Maybe the lack of sleep is getting to you."

Unbeknownst to Denise, Jesus had appeared on the sand near them. The wind snapped his robe.

Savannah drew in her breath sharply, startled by his unexpected arrival.

Denise wondered what was wrong, watching her sister stare off into space.

Without any formalities, Jesus said to Savannah, "Ask your sister about the lump on Blanca's leg."

She did as he instructed, saying to Denise, "Jesus told me to ask you about the lump on Blanca's leg."

"How did you know?" Denise was confused.

"Tell her it's gone now," Jesus said.

"Denise, Jesus says the lump is gone."

"What?" She looked at her dog, who was digging a hole in the sand, shouting, "Blanca, come here!"

The Bichon Frise sprinted over to her.

Denise set Blanca on her lap, then ran her fingers over the dog's leg, repeatedly searching for the lump that was no longer there. She finally sighed with relief when she couldn't find it, embracing Blanca and crying with joy. Then she lifted her face toward the sky, yelling at the top of her lungs, "Thank you, Jesus!"

Savannah looked up before pointing out, "You know, he's standing right next me."

Denise exclaimed, "He's everywhere!" She laughed with delight.

CHAPTER 12

Temporary Peace

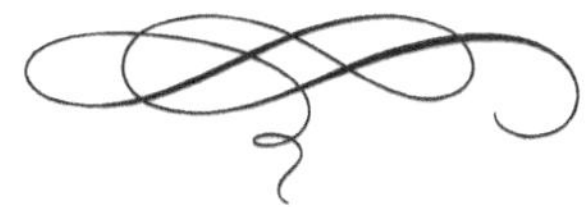

STEVE WAS GRILLING CHICKEN despite the gloomy weather and strong winds. He waved the smoke away from his face as he teased Savannah, who sat at the patio table, saying to her, "All those doves made me hungry!"

"Ha, ha," she said, pretending to laugh.

Then, trying to sound casual, Steve mentioned, "Maybe we should head home today and forfeit my day off tomorrow. It's supposed to be cold and wet anyway."

His suggestion made Savannah apprehensive. Because of the dream, she dreaded driving the family home. "You know traffic is terrible on Sundays."

"Not if we head out after lunch."

"I don't think it's a good idea," she insisted. "Let me know when the food's ready." She got up without an explanation, walking inside the house.

Savannah went up to her bedroom. She sat on the bed wondering how to deal with the inevitable departure. The house had become both a haven and a prison. A haven because everyone was safe here. And a prison because she was afraid to leave it, at least with the family in tow. She called out, "Jesus, I need to talk to you—"

Instantly, he was sitting on the other side of the bed.

Pleased by his prompt appearance, she greeted him, "Hi. Thanks for coming."

"I never left you."

"Sorry, I keep forgetting." She paused before asking the question that she wasn't sure she wanted the answer to, "Can you tell me if it's safe to drive home today?"

"You are always safe."

He hadn't answered her question. At least she didn't think so. Her irritation caused her voice to be harsher than she intended. "Jesus, I can't handle riddles about how my spirit lives forever. Not right now. I just need to know if my family will die in a car crash...driving home... today."

Jesus comforted her. "You are trying to make the dream real. And dreams are always dreams."

Could it be that simple? Was it simply a dream? Savannah asked herself. But then the dream's images flashed through her mind. She countered, "But this dream is different. It's persistent and vivid. It feels very real."

"Perceptions are tricky. Everyone sees from his or her own vantage point. What you experience will always depend on your frame of mind. If you believe in death, you will experience death."

"You expect me to believe that it's possible to avoid death by changing my beliefs?"

"What is immortal can never die. You will remain as God created you for all of eternity. Unchangeable. Forever. Your spirit's voyage through this world has no bearing on its reality, no matter what seems to transpire here."

Transpire? What a gruesome word. One that filled her with dread. She demanded to know, "Just tell me! Is it safe to drive home!?"

"Again, there is no death, only dreams of dying," Jesus stated.

"Why can't you just answer my question? I feel like strangling you right now," she seethed.

"This would be a great time to offer your fears and unloving thoughts to the Holy Spirit for healing."

Savannah's anger unfurled. "The way you dodged my question, you should have been a politician!"

"Again, you have it backwards. You have dodged the answer," Jesus said, then vanished from her sight.

The clouds had floated away, leaving the beach exposed under the afternoon sun—a brief respite from the expected evening storm.

Denise lay on an orange-striped towel sunbathing while her little dog chased the seagulls.

Steve and the kids were boogie boarding, always looking for the perfect wave.

Savannah sat on the deck under the patio umbrella that rattled in the strengthening breeze. She had calmed down after the unsettling conversation with Jesus, mostly because she had decided that she and the kids would stay another week here, avoiding the trip home altogether. This decision provided a temporary, but much needed, sense of peace. She closed her eyes and listened to the roar of the ocean, shrieking seagulls, and the chatter of voices echoing from the beach. She could almost remember how perfect life had been before the dream had begun to torment her.

A solitary gust of wind blew across the shore, whipping over the dunes, spiraling up to where she sat, stinging her face with its salty breath. She kept her eyes closed, embracing the moment. The wind. The water.

The clear skies. Everything flowed in synchronicity—a universal dance card that held everyone's name. When she opened her eyes, the water was bluer than ever. The sand sparkled like diamonds.

Wet with salt water, Emily and Justin headed up the deck stairs, radiating so brilliantly that their bodies appeared almost translucent. The children had never seemed more beautiful and innocent to Savannah, who got up to hug and kiss them, one after the other.

"Mom! What's gotten into you?" Emily wiped off the kiss, pretending not to like it.

"What about me?" asked Steve, who wasn't far behind the kids. Towels were slung over his shoulder. Savannah kissed him on the lips. He grinned, then called out to the kids, "Shower off before you go inside!"

The radiant light faded from view, but Savannah's spirit continued to glow inside her.

CHAPTER 13

Denise

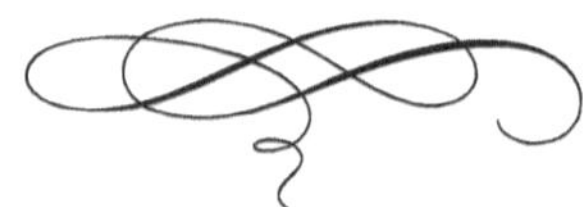

SAVANNAH WOKE UP IN the hospital room. Her sister and father appeared as fuzzy figures talking quietly between themselves. Not realizing she was injured, Savannah decided to change positions, hoping to alleviate the intense ache that coursed throughout her body, but the instant she moved, pain burst from her broken legs. She cried out in agony.

Denise rushed over, saying, "It's okay. We're here."

Savannah remained perfectly still, careful not to antagonize her pain, asking in a raspy strained voice, "Where am I?"

Denise's heart tightened. "You're in the hospital. You're going to be okay."

"What happened?"

Although grateful that Savannah was awake, Denise had been dreading this moment. She steeled herself before answering her sister's question, "You were in a car accident."

"How long have I been here?"

"It's been a week."

"Where are the kids? And Steve?"

Denise envisioned her sister's life crashing down before her eyes, and she didn't want to be the messenger.

Her hesitation made Savannah afraid. "Are they here? Tell me they're okay!"

"I wish I could. More than anything in the world, but the accident was too severe. They died instantly. There wasn't any pain—"

"Noooo!" Savannah began to shake. "No! It's not true! I was just with them. This morning at the beach. You were there. You know it's true! You know they're fine. Don't you?"

Denise glanced at their dad for help, but he sat in the recliner with his head hanging low, unable to deal with his daughter's pain.

Savannah, remaining in denial, said, "This morning was wonderful. A bit cool, but we had fun...and Jesus was there."

Denise raised her eyebrows with concern. *Okay,* she thought, *Now she's seeing Jesus. She has to be hallucinating.*

"You remember," Savannah persisted. "You were there when Jesus said Blanca's lump was gone. You were thrilled about it."

Denise was shocked by her sister's words. A biopsy was scheduled for the lump on Blanca's leg, but she hadn't told Savannah about it, because it had been discovered just before the accident occurred. *Maybe Savannah overheard me telling Dad or Carol,* Denise speculated. *They say people in comas can hear you.* To pacify her sister, she responded, "Of course, Blanca's fine. Everything is going to be okay."

"Yes, they're all fine. I'm going to the beach. Are you coming?" Savannah's eyes fluttered shut.

"Um...I'll be there in a minute," Denise answered with tears streaming down her face.

Denise drove on Interstate 40 with the Fiat's convertible top down. The wind flowed over the windshield, caressing her sun-infused skin. She didn't want to think. Or feel. She just wanted to drive.

A truck driver blasted his horn, shocking her out of her peaceful oblivion. She looked up before she could stop herself.

The truck driver blew her a kiss.

Denise cringed, sick of it all. She punched the gas,

leaving the obnoxious truck driver behind, wishing she was already home.

A half-hour later, she drove over the expansive bridge that offered a scenic view of Wilmington's historic homes and the commercial district nestled along the inlet off the Atlantic Ocean.

Denise ventured into the city. After a few lights, she turned right onto a street shaded by majestic oak trees. Up ahead was a notable mansion with plantation columns and a balcony that spanned the front. The old house had been converted into four apartments before the Historic Preservation Commission began limiting these types of remodeling projects. Denise knew she was lucky to have the place, and always made sure her rent was paid on time.

The compact car jostled as it moved over the uneven cobblestone driveway. When it passed under a second-story window, Denise looked up and saw Blanca bouncing and barking with joy. The woman waved her arm in the air, giving her furry companion a warm welcome.

After parking in her designated spot, Denise grabbed her stuff, hit the button to close the convertible top, then got out, walking toward the exposed wooden staircase that ran up the side of the manor.

Her neighbor, Mildred, an older and somewhat nosy

woman, was putting trash bags in the bin. She called out, "Denise! How's your sister doing?"

Unable to answer without crying, Denise shook her head and kept climbing the steps.

Mildred called after her, "Let me know if you need anything."

Denise reached the landing, swinging the door open, dropping her purse inside. The Bichon Frise sprung into her arms, wiggling and covering her with wet kisses. It was just what the woman needed. "Oh, you're such a good girl," she cooed, absorbing Blanca's love, but it still wasn't enough to lift the burden of the recent tragedies.

She lay on the sofa with the little dog nuzzled beside her. The last remnants of sunlight streamed through the window, engulfing the two of them.

After a moment, Denise remembered what Savannah had said about Jesus healing the lump on her dog's leg. *Could it be true?* She gently stretched out Blanca's small leg, tenderly probing the skin under the curly white hair. The Bichon Frise enjoyed the impromptu massage.

Denise couldn't find the lump.

She searched again and again, finally saying to Blanca, "Where did it go? This is so odd." The little dog tilted her head trying to understand her mistress, who contemplated out loud, "What if Savannah really did talk to Jesus? Maybe she had a near-death experience or something. But why would he heal your leg when she's lost her whole family? Oh, my God, I'm losing it. Now I'm buying into her delusions. But where did the lump go?" Her mind couldn't rationalize it.

Numb and overwhelmed, Denise went into the bathroom, going directly to the clawfoot tub. She turned the chrome knobs, sprinkled bath salts over the gushing water, then let her clothes drop to the floor.

The exhausted woman slowly immersed herself in the hot bath. Steam filled the small room, creating a womb where she felt safe. Her phone, still tucked in her purse in the other room, rang out a muffled tone. She began to cry. The deaths, Savannah's injuries, her father's heart attack, and Blanca's cancer scare were too much for her to deal with, and it still wasn't over—not until the veterinarian confirmed the lump was gone.

Blanca peeked over the edge of the tub, her pink tongue hanging out.

"Do you believe in miracles?" Denise asked softly.

The dog wagged her tail.

CHAPTER 14
Denial

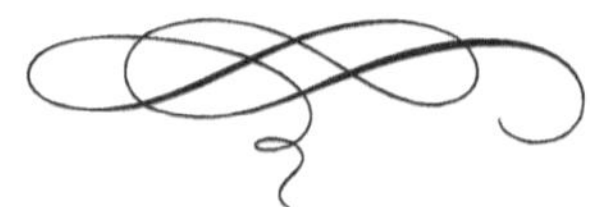

SAVANNAH, WHO WAS CONSCIOUS for longer and longer periods, stared out the hospital window at a solitary dogwood tree planted beside the sidewalk. "Trees are meant to be in forests," she said, mostly to herself.

Denise lifted her head from a magazine. "What?"

"Have you ever wondered why we're here? There's so much pain. Too much pain."

Denise stared at her sister, not knowing how to respond.

"They're not dead," Savannah stated, never looking away from the tree.

Not wanting to argue or risk upsetting her sister, Denise replied, "It's all right."

Savannah continued with her introspective ramblings,

"Everything's so dark here."

Denise sat mutely until Savannah asked her, "Can you get my straw hat? I want to go for a walk."

Confused, Denise replied, "Where do you want to go? Down the hall?"

"To the beach," she uttered before closing her eyes, falling asleep.

CHAPTER 15

The Stars and Moon

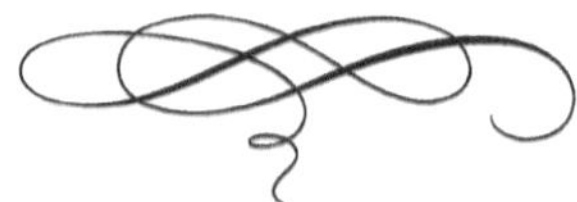

THE WATSON FAMILY WAS eating their Sunday dinner inside at the dining table. It was too dreary and chilly to eat on the deck. The Portabella mushroom sandwiches and seasoned vegetables that Savannah had prepared were not a hit with the children. They picked through the healthy fare looking for something edible.

Steve said, "I've decided I'm definitely going to work tomorrow. I don't want to use my vacation time if it's going to rain."

Savannah nodded her head in agreement, then spoke the words she had rehearsed earlier, "I'm going to stay here with the kids. It's the end of summer and there aren't many days left."

"Will you be okay without a car?"

"Sure."

"What if you have that dream?"

"I'll be fine."

"What are we suppose to do if it's raining?" Justin complained.

"How about something creative?" his mother answered. "Use your imagination. I mean it. I'm only allowing one hour of TV or video games tomorrow. You'll have to entertain—"

"That's not fair!" Justin shouted.

"Young man, we don't shout at people. Do you understand?"

He mumbled under his breath.

"I couldn't hear you."

"Yes, ma'am."

"To help clear your thinking, you get to clean the table."

Justin complained under his breath.

Savannah warned him, "If I hear any more, you'll spend the rest of the night in your room."

Her son grabbed his plate, stacking it on top of another one, then stomped to the sink.

Emily smirked, pleased that her brother was in trouble.

Steve looked out the window, studying the sky. "It's

getting dark. Think I'll head out now to beat the storm."

"All right," Savannah agreed. "So we'll see you Friday?"

"Sounds good." He kissed her on the cheek.

Later that night, the storm that Steve had mentioned earlier rolled across the ocean. Rain pelted the windows. Savannah sat in the living room gazing out the sliding glass door at the flashes of lightning and the turbulent waves crashing against the shore, leaving behind a trail of foam.

There was a knock at the door.

Savannah thought it was strange that anyone would be out in this weather. Then fear struck her. *How long had it been since Steve had left?* She hurried toward the door, nearly knocking over the lamp on the end table, all the while dreading the possibility of a police officer standing on the other side, ready to deliver bad news.

But when the door opened, she saw a woman holding an umbrella, obscured by the darkness and rain.

The woman talked loudly, her voice rising above the weather, "My son is missing! If you see him, please call me." She pulled a sheet off the stack of flyers she held while precariously balancing her umbrella. She handed the flyer to Savannah. "Please call me if you see him!"

"I will," she promised.

The woman nodded, then rushed down the stairs and into the storm.

Savannah went back inside, sitting on the sofa near the lamp where she examined the damp flyer. A photo of a young boy with a toothless smile stared back at her. His name "Tyler Wyndale" was in big letters underneath. Savannah's heart sank as she imagined how desperate his mother must feel—even the elements were conspiring against her.

Jesus appeared on the sofa sitting next to Savannah, who, in a strange way, had expected his arrival.

She looked at him. "Would you please help this boy? Please."

"Of course, but this is something we can do together."

"Together?" Savannah asked, confused.

"Yes. When I was quoted in the Bible as saying, 'All that I have done, you can do and more,' I meant it."

"But how?"

"First, relax."

Savannah settled into the sofa.

Then Jesus instructed, "Now quiet your mind. Once it is still, the answers will come. They may present themselves as a knowing in your heart, a whisper in your ear, or a vision of insight. Just sit quietly and wait."

Savannah closed her eyes and let her mind be receptive to Divine insight. The urgency of the situation helped her to focus.

Flashes of random scenes began to appear. At first, they seemed unrelated, but soon came together to weave a story. The boy's mother walked into a bedroom, surprised that it was empty. Next, the mother and others were seen searching the beach, calling out the boy's name. Then Savannah saw the missing boy struggling through gusts of wind and rain as he walked along a dark street. He approached a raised beach house, sneaking past the ground-level lattice, and then in between the concrete columns that supported the structure, seeking refuge from the storm.

With her eyes still closed, Savannah told Jesus, "I see the boy. He's scared and hiding under a house."

"Ask him why he is there."

Savannah spoke to the boy in her vision, "Tyler?"

He turned toward her.

Surprised that he so calmly accepted her presence, she asked him, "Why aren't you home?"

"I wanted to watch the storm. I didn't go in the water."

"Of course not," she assured him.

"But I couldn't tell the houses apart..." He tried not to cry.

"I know...it's different at night, isn't it?"

Tyler nodded.

"Why didn't you ask for help?"

"My mom told me not to talk to strangers."

Savannah smiled at the irony of him talking to her now. Then, behind Tyler, through the lattice, she noticed the pier in the distance, and despite the murkiness of night, she recognized it. It was the same one—

Her heart beat wildly. To confirm her belief, she double-checked the bikes and boogie boards propped against the cement-block supporting wall. These were her items.

The boy was standing in her garage.

In the living room, Savannah cried out, "Oh, my God!"

She jumped up, running out the door and down the stairs through the rain, heading into the garage beneath the house. She flipped on the light, looking past the bikes and beach toys.

The boy, who was clinging to the lattice, watching the storm with wonder and fear, was startled and turned toward her.

Savannah approached him, coming close enough to hold a conversation, yet staying a safe distance away so she wouldn't spook him. "Tyler, it's all right. Your mother is looking for you. Let's call her. Okay? She'll come get you."

He nodded his head.

Savannah held out her hand.

Tyler sheepishly stepped toward her, taking it.

They went up the stairs, pelted by rain, going into the house. As soon as the door closed, the storm's fury seemed miles away.

Savannah invited Tyler to sit at the dining table, then went into the living room to grab the flyer.

She made the call.

A woman's voice answered, "Hello." It was difficult to hear her.

"Mrs. Wyndale?"

"Yes?" Tyler's mother stood on a landing farther down the street, pressing her finger against her exposed ear to block the storm's noise.

"I have your son. He's safe."

The woman cried from relief. "Where...you?" The call broke up.

"Forty-three twenty-five Island Drive."

"What!? I didn't hear you!" she desperately shouted.

"Forty-three twenty-five Island Drive. Did you get it?"

"Yes! I'll be right there!"

Savannah went into the kitchen, telling Tyler, "She'll be here in a minute."

The boy smiled.

Jesus approached Tyler, putting his unfelt hand on the boy's shoulder.

Savannah smiled at Jesus with gratitude.

A moment later, the knock came.

Savannah went to answer it. The boy followed her.

When the door opened, Mrs. Wyndale immediately locked eyes with her son, moving past Savannah without saying a word. The mother leaned down to embrace Tyler, her umbrella dripping over the floor.

After a moment, the mother stood up, saying to Savannah, "Thank you, so much. Where was he? He's barely wet."

"I found him in our garage."

"What a relief. We were scared to death Tyler had gone in the water," she shuddered, "but, thank God, he's all right."

Savannah said, "I'm so glad I found him when I did, otherwise, he might have stayed out all night, alone."

Mrs. Wyndale said to Tyler, "You did the right thing, getting somewhere safe, kiddo, but it's time to go. I've got some calls to make."

She turned toward Savannah, saying, "This is an answer to my prayers. Many prayers. Thank you, again."

The mother held up the umbrella, using it to cover her son as they headed out the door.

Savannah turned toward Jesus, saying, "Well, that turned out pretty good. Life doesn't usually offer that quick of a resolution."

They walked to the sofa together, sitting down, silently watching the storm.

Suddenly, a lightning bolt seared through the night sky, lighting up the dark ocean. Thunder exploded, rattling the house.

The kids came out of their rooms, their footsteps heard on the floor above.

Justin shouted in the upper hallway, "Mom!"

"Down here!" Savannah answered loudly.

The kids scurried down the stairs, going to their mother, snuggling on each side of her where they felt safe. Once settled, they all stared out at the storm.

Lighting flashed again.

Emily counted the seconds until the thunder was heard. "Two seconds means its two miles away," she declared fearlessly, now that her mother was by her side.

The storm continued its pattern of lightning followed by thunder as it rolled into the distance, the repetition lulling everyone to sleep.

Savannah began dreaming. Flashes of lightning turned into reflective white lines rushing down the center of a two-lane highway. Steve was driving the family through the night. She heard the tires cutting through the standing rainwater. A deer stood in the middle of the road. Brakes screeched. Their SUV skidded. An oncoming car swerved. Its headlights came closer to them, encompassing the windshield.

Time moved in slow motion.

Savannah heard the collision.

The windshield shattered, splintering into a thousand pieces.

The airbags deployed, front and rear.

They should have been safe, but headlights approached their SUV from behind, filling the interior.

The sound of the second impact was deafening.

Savannah's head slammed against the headrest before bounding forward.

Everything went black.

Then the nightmare ended.

Savannah woke up breathing heavily and sweating. She glanced at the kids pressed against her. They were asleep. Her analytical mind was relieved the accident wasn't real, but she couldn't shake the painful emotions that had accompanied the dream. Those felt real. She began crying.

Jesus, who had not left Savannah's side, understood her pain. He assured her, "Everything is all right."

She asked softly so she wouldn't rouse the children, "Why won't it stop? Everything is ruined by this horrible dream—over and over."

"Let's go outside," Jesus suggested.

"I don't want to go out there in this weather."

"Trust me. It will be okay." Jesus stood up, and then extended his hand.

Savannah relented, accepting his help, slowly getting up. The sleeping kids slumped into her vacant spot.

Jesus pulled open the sliding glass door, motioning for her to go first.

They walked across the deck. The rain poured over them.

Jesus led her down the steps and over the sand to where the furious waves flung themselves against the shore, their white caps reflecting in the moonlight.

It took a tremendous amount of faith on Savannah's part to follow him into the dangerous waters that pushed and tugged against their legs. She unconsciously squeezed his hand tighter, afraid of the strong current pulling her under. "This would be a great time to walk on the water instead of in it," she said light-heartedly, although she was serious.

"Just feel it," Jesus instructed her. "The wind, the water, the power, the energy force behind the storm. Just let it flow through you without fear, without thought. Just feel it."

She felt herself connect to the elements, momentarily becoming dizzy, tightening her grip on his hand to steady herself. The cold rain ran down her face. The waves wrapped themselves around her legs and waist. She heard the wind sing sadly like a forgotten lover calling to its lost mate. The roar of the ocean waves synchronized with her heartbeat. The thunder vibrated throughout her body. She felt the rhythm of the storm. She called to it, then heard it answer. And as she listened, the storm felt understood and loved. Slowly, the winds calmed and the rain lightened, eventually ceasing.

She smiled at Jesus, exclaiming, "That was beautiful! I want more!"

Instantly, they were out of the earth's atmosphere, floating in space, looking down at the planet, one half cloaked in darkness while the other half gloriously displayed its oceans and landmasses frosted with swirling clouds.

They soared toward the cratered moon.

Savannah spoke to the large gray orb, asking how it felt about its companion, earth.

The moon let Savannah feel its connection with the planet—an intimate communication pulsing back and forth—a loving game of tug of war.

Then the stars called to her, singing a sweet familiar song. The volume grew louder as the infinite number of stars sang in unison from the deep recesses of the galaxy. The planets joined in, adding a beat like a bass player in a jazz band. She laughed at their silliness, their playfulness.

Jesus began leading Savannah back to earth.

As they went, she proclaimed to the universe, "I love you!"

A child-like laughter rang out, answering, "We love you, too!"

While the Son of God and the woman traveled back through earth's atmosphere, Savannah's body shook and trembled until they passed through its powerful force, descending below the clouds, watching the sun make its rounds.

Her hand slipped from his. Savannah plunged into the ocean, sinking beneath the rolling waves, air bubbles surrounding her as she twisted in the saltwater, unsure of which way to swim until she saw the glow from the sunrise dancing on the surface.

She swam up and up, using the light as her guide, bursting into the air, welcomed by the sun peeking its head over the horizon.

Although not entirely comfortable being this far from

land, she swam on her back watching the stars disappear into the morning sky. The barest whisper of their hymn could still be heard, for just a moment, and then it was gone.

The waves didn't become troublesome until Savannah neared the beach where they surged and curled. She struggled through the surf, reaching the shore.

Her pilgrimage had ended.

She stood at the water's edge, her wet hair dripping over her shoulders.

An elderly couple, who were taking an early stroll, curiously stared at the fully clothed, yet soaked, woman standing beside the ocean.

Savannah raised her arms, shouting at the heavens, "I love you!"

The couple quickened their steps, moving past her.

CHAPTER 16
Finding a Lawyer

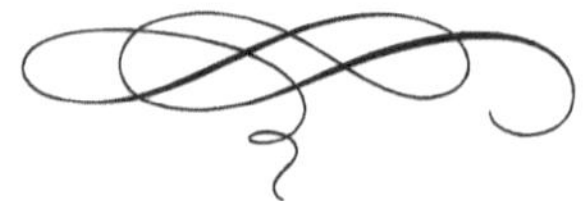

BECAUSE OF HER IMPROVEMENT, Savannah had been moved out of the Critical Care Unit and into a private room, but her mental condition remained of high concern to her surviving family members. Every mention of her children and husband's deaths were met with denial, and caused her to sink deeper into her own fantasy world. The nurses remained attentive, checking her vitals and administering the medications, and slowly Savannah's body mended, but the family doubted she would be able to deal with reality anytime soon. Which is why Denise, Carol and Herman were walking down an office corridor searching for an attorney.

"What's the name again?" Herman asked.

"I told you, I can't remember the whole name," Carol

answered, annoyed by the question, which had already been asked in the car and lobby. "It starts with Finch. The directory said it was office number three-seventeen."

They came upon a frosted-glass door with the name Finch, Lynchman & Grunter painted in gold letters. They stepped inside.

The young woman minding the desk greeted them, "Good afternoon. Your name please?"

The trio looked at each other, unsure of who should take the lead. Finally, Herman spoke up, "We're here to see a Mr. Finch for Savannah Watson."

"Please, sit down. Mr. Finch will be with you in a moment." She picked up the phone to notify her boss that his clients had arrived.

Although he wasn't busy, Mr. Finch sat at his desk scrolling through social media for another ten minutes before he buzzed his receptionist, telling her to escort the clients into his office.

The family entered. The attorney stood up to shake Herman's hand over his desk. After everyone was seated, he asked them to describe their situation.

Denise told Mr. Finch about the car accident, the loss of their family members, her sister's state of mind and seeming inability to accept the deaths of her loved ones. Meanwhile, there were insurance claims that needed to be submitted so they could pay for the funerals, and medical and eventual rehabilitation expenses on her behalf.

"Is either of you Savannah's parent?" asked Mr. Finch.

Herman cleared his throat and answered, "I am."

"Good. We'll ask the court to set up a trust for Savannah in your name. If she is deemed incapable, and you're approved, you'll have the authority to file claims, make funeral arrangements and take care of Savannah's needs. I can handle all of this for you," Mr. Finch offered. "It will take a considerable burden off your shoulders."

Herman was distrustful of everyone, but especially lawyers. He responded to the lawyer's offer by saying, "We'll see."

Mr. Finch acted as if he hadn't heard the rebuff and continued, "I'll also take a look at the police report to see if you have a wrongful death claim, although I highly recommend we start our own investigation now. Did you bring the auto and life insurance policies with you?"

Denise handed the paperwork to him.

Mr. Finch skimmed the pages. "There's an accidental death clause in the life insurance, which doubles the face amount. That makes her husband's insurance policy worth one million dollars." His eyes gleamed as he said it, but he managed to contain his excitement, commenting, "She'll be well taken care of."

The lawyer's expression annoyed Herman, who fidgeted a moment, then gruffly said to Carol and Denise, "I don't trust this greedy blood-sucking parasite. I'm leaving!" He stood up, walking out the door.

Denise and Carol were dumbfounded by his outburst, but they saw no reason to stay. Denise grabbed the papers off Mr. Finch's desk.

Both women followed Herman into the hallway where Carol asked him why he had reacted so negatively to the attorney.

"I don't trust him, that's why. We'll find another one. It can't be too hard. This building's full of 'em."

Herman started walking down the hall, looking at the names on the doors. He stopped in front of one marked, "Beatrice Hardman, P.A.–Wills, Trusts and Guardianships."

They entered the office.

A receptionist in her mid-40s occupied the desk. She smiled at them, asking with a sweet southern drawl, "Can I help y'all?"

Herman said, "We would like to meet with Beatrice Hardman...to see if we like her...as an attorney."

"Do you have an appointment?"

"No."

"We normally require an appointment."

"Well, then, we'll have to continue our search," Herman curtly responded.

The unseen Ms. Hardman called out from behind her closed office door, "Give me five minutes!"

The receptionist acted as if she heard nothing, politely saying, "She'll be with you in a moment. Please have a seat."

After a few minutes, they were escorted into the attorney's office.

Ms. Hardman was a plump woman wearing a plain sensible dress suit. She got out of her leather chair, coming around her desk to shake their hands, then asked them to sit at the small conference table near the window.

Once seated, Herman explained the situation to her. The attorney made notes on her legal pad, and at one point, offered her condolences. When he was finished, Ms. Hardman listed their options and the possible outcomes. She really didn't have any new information to add beyond what the first lawyer had given them, but Herman was comfortable with her, which was a relief to Carol and Denise. And since Ms. Hardman could start the process immediately, it wouldn't be long before they could bury their loved ones and have some closure.

CHAPTER 17

Rosewood

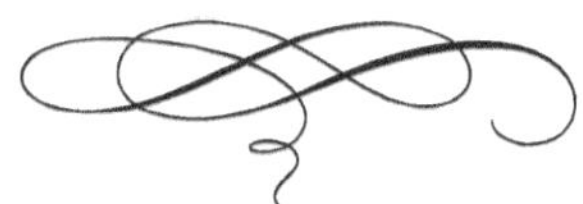

THREE WEEKS LATER, SAVANNAH was in a wheelchair being pushed down a corridor at the Rosewood Rehabilitation Center. After convalescing in a hospital bed for so long, the movement caused her equilibrium to spin. The male attendant entered a reception area, speaking to the woman behind the desk, then he wheeled Savannah through an office door that stood open, parking her beside the leather couch.

The attendant locked the wheels, saying to her, "I'll be back in an hour," then he left.

After Savannah's head stopped spinning, she glanced around the room, noticing a bookcase filled with reference books, and a middle-aged man who sat at a walnut-stained desk. Behind him was a window offering a splendid view of the well-tended lawn below.

The man waited until she looked directly at him, then he said to her, "Good afternoon."

"Good afternoon," she replied.

"My name is Doctor Martin. How are you today?"

"Dizzy, tired and in constant pain, but other than that, I'm fine."

"Well, I hope you feel better soon. Do you know why you're here?"

"To recover."

"Yes. Well, I'm here to help you with any emotional concerns you may have. No matter how big or small. We can discuss whatever's on your mind." He waited for her to say something, but she sat staring out the window. He cleared his throat, beginning the conversation, "So, besides your aches and pains, what else concerns you?"

Slowly, and without emotion, Savannah answered, "I'm plagued by this dream."

"A dream? Can you describe it?"

She extended her hand, motioning around the room, "This one."

"You mean, right now?" Dr. Martin asked, trying to hide his astonishment. He had read the previous doctor's notes in her file, but he found her comment disconcerting nonetheless, especially since she seemed cognitive otherwise.

"Yes, right now."

"Let me make sure I understand. You're saying that this very moment is a dream. Is that correct?"

"Yes."

"Can you tell me why you believe it's a dream?"

"Because in my real life, I'm dreaming of this one."

That was a mind bender. To gather his thoughts, the doctor wrote something on his notepad, then asked, "Can you tell me more about your real life?"

"Sure. My family lives in Garner, North Carolina, but during the summer, we spend most of our weekends at our beach house on Topsail Island. It's beautiful there. Clean sand, small town."

Dr. Martin nodded, sympathizing with Savannah who, because of her family's recent deaths, had obviously detached from reality and preferred living in the past. He asked her, "What can you tell me about this dream?"

"Well..." She looked around the room. "It goes on and on...like a serial nightmare."

"And when you wake up, you believe you'll be with your family at the beach house, correct?"

"Yes."

"So what do you think the dream's purpose is?

"I'm not entirely sure. Maybe it's a warning."

"Would you agree that it's unusual for a dream to last so long and appear to be so real?"

"Yes."

"Are you sure this life is a dream, and not the other way around?"

"What do you mean?"

"Well, how should I put this? What if your life at the beach house is the dream?"

This comment caused a fear to surge inside Savannah that was so enormous it threatened to devour her. Tears trickled out of her eyes.

Dr. Martin immediately regretted his blunt question, gently saying, "I'm sorry...that was callous of me. Please forgive me."

Savannah grabbed a tissue off the end table.

The doctor said nothing while she composed herself.

She dried her tears, then rested her hands on her lap, staring numbly at the carpet. The doctor's comment whirled around her mind until she thought, *No, he's not right. He couldn't be.* Savannah harnessed his comment, locking it away. Her fiery disposition returned. She asked the doctor, "How do *you* know this life isn't a dream?"

The question caught him off guard.

She challenged him, "Prove to me this life is real!"

"I'm not sure I could *prove* to you this life is real."

"Try," she insisted.

"Well...I can feel my desk." Dr. Martin said, running his hand over it. "I ate lunch a little while ago. I caught my toenail on my sock this morning, and it still hurts."

Savannah responded, "All of those things can happen in a dream, and feel real while they are happening."

Dr. Martin felt the session was slipping out of his control. "Yes, but when you wake up, you realize it was just a dream."

"Then I just haven't woken up yet," she said matter-of-factly. "You can't prove this life is real, and science can't prove this life is real."

Her latest comment hit a nerve in the doctor, who held strong beliefs in scientific and medical explanations. "I'm sure science can prove this life is real."

"No, it can't," said Savannah, shaking her head. "Scientists can dissect a brain, yet they don't know where thoughts come from. They can trace our DNA, but can't prove our origin."

Dr. Martin responded, "I know I'm probably going to regret this, but...the Big Bang has been accepted by the science community as the creation of the universe."

"Who or what created the Big Bang?"

Dr. Martin remained mute. He knew that no one could answer that question without resorting to faith or an unproven theory.

Savannah continued, "You can't prove this life is real, and my only hope for not losing my mind is to believe this life is a dream."

The irony was not lost on Dr. Martin, who believed she had already lost touch with reality.

After the therapy session ended, the attendant wheeled Savannah outside onto the courtyard where she could view the gardens and lawn that sloped toward the road. Her insurance money had allowed her to reside in a very nice rehabilitation center. The other patients sat on wrought-iron patio chairs enjoying the great outdoors under the watchful eyes of two male orderlies standing nearby.

Flowering Crepe Myrtle trees swayed back and forth in the breeze, and beneath them in the beds were rose bushes and cannas—a collective spectacle meant to impress the relatives of prospective patients.

A male patient came over. He stood next to Savannah, introducing himself, "Hi, I'm Sam."

Although she didn't want to be bothered, she answered politely, "Hello, I'm Savannah."

He said, "I've never seen you before. You must be new here." He didn't wait for her response. "Me? I've been here almost a year."

"That's a long time."

"Yep. Not sure when I'm getting out, but when I do, I'm going to live in the woods, right over there." Sam raised his hand, pointing to the small forest at the edge of the center's property. "Seen some deer there once." He unexpectedly shouted at the open air, "Shut up! I'm trying to talk to the lady."

Shocked, Savannah watched Sam wander away, talking to himself, weaving between the other patients. For the first time, she took a good hard look at the residents on the courtyard. One young man sitting in a wheelchair seemed like he might be there for rehabilitation, but the others stared aimlessly or rocked back and forth. Was this a glorified mental ward?

The young man had noticed Savannah glancing his way and wheeled himself over to her to start a conversation. "This is some place," he said. "One minute I'm enjoying a bike ride and the next thing I know, I wake up in a hospital with no idea what happened."

"Sorry to hear that."

"Thanks. My name's Garret Barnes."

"Savannah Watson."

"The sun sure feels good, doesn't it?"

"Yes. It's been way too long since I've been in it."

"You a sun worshipper?"

"Definitely. I live for the beach."

"Well, hopefully, you'll get back there soon."

Savannah remembered the golden days with her family. Dinners on the deck. Boogie boarding. Sand castles. But when her mind returned to the present moment, the pain of being separate from her loved ones was too heavy of a burden to bear. She needed to lay down. "Well, I'm tired. I'm going to head back to my room and rest," she told him.

"Would you like me to walk with you?" Then Garret remembered the two of them were in wheelchairs. He laughed at his oversight, flashing a radiant smile, which lightened Savannah's mood a little. He clarified, "Well, actually roll would be more like it."

She gripped her wheelchair's push-rims, attempting to move forward, but she ended up spinning in one direction, and then another, going nowhere. Frustrated, she glanced at the orderlies wondering if one would help her, but neither looked her way so she concentrated, slowly moving forward.

Garret cautiously rolled beside her. "It's tough in the beginning, but it gets easier. I've been here two weeks, not a veteran by any means, but I've come a long ways."

His happy-go-lucky attitude sucked Savannah into the conversation. While turning the wheels, she mentioned, "I start rehab tomorrow."

"They're good here. At least I think so. I've gotten therapy for my back and leg, but there are a lot of patients here who aren't right in the head."

Savannah didn't respond, thinking about her earlier session with Dr. Martin. She pushed the red button on the exterior wall. The glass door automatically opened. She propelled the wheelchair down the hall, her arms shaking at the effort.

"You're getting the hang of it," Garret said, trying to encourage her.

But his words had the opposite effect. Savannah's heart became heavy because it seemed that every character in this dream believed in its reality. But for her, it was an exercise in futility—at least until the dream ended.

She was exhausted by the time they reached her room. "Well, here's my temporary home. It was nice meeting you." She punched the numbers on the keypad, unlocking the door, then clumsily maneuvered the wheelchair past the threshold.

Garret tried to hold the door open for her, but found it difficult to reach past his wheelchair and hers.

Somewhat flustered, Savannah finally got inside. Over her shoulder, she called back, "Thank you."

"See you around," he said as the door slowly closed.

CHAPTER 18
Fantastical Journey

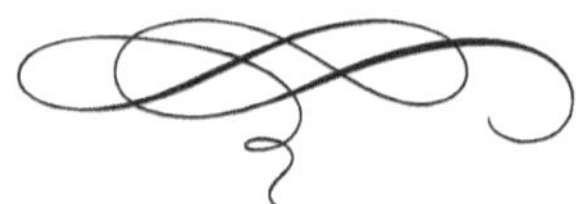

DENISE PARKED IN FRONT of the veterinarian's office. "Here we are, Blanca. Your favorite place."

Blanca whimpered and cowered in her doggy seat.

Denise unbuckled the strap and placed the little dog inside a carrier, telling her in a soothing voice, "It's going to be okay."

Fifteen minutes later, Dr. Sullivan examined the trembling Bichon Frise, searching for the lump that was no longer there. After numerous attempts, and with a puzzled expression on her face, the veterinarian finally conceded, "Well, she appears to be perfectly healthy. Obviously, the lump wasn't cancerous since it went away. Looks like we avoided an unnecessary biopsy."

"What a relief. What was it?" asked Denise, who

scooped Blanca into her arms.

"I don't know. It's uncommon for a hard lump to disappear, but let's be grateful that it did."

Blanca kept tilting her head, trying to understand what was being said about her.

Denise ruffled the little dog's hair, stating, "You're going to be with me a long time, girl. What do you say about that?"

Blanca wagged her tail and let out a high-pitched bark.

Both Denise and Dr. Sullivan laughed.

Savannah was in the kitchen putting away dishes when the phone rang. "Hello?"

"Hey! Guess what!" Denise said enthusiastically.

"What?"

"I'm driving back from the vet's office and she said there's no lump!"

"I thought we already knew that."

"Well, I wanted to get it confirmed by a professional. Okay? Anyway, Blanca was declared healed."

"We'll have to celebrate, but this time, you bring the steaks," Savannah suggested, alluding to the fact that Denise often mooched their food.

"Hey! I buy lots of stuff for you guys."

"Like?" Savannah countered.

"I'm thinking. Wait...well, I know I do...I just can't think of anything right now."

"Um-huh." Savannah rubbed it in, but she really didn't mind if Denise contributed to the "food pot" or not.

"I'll bring the steaks next time. Right now, I can't, because I just paid the vet bill."

"But you knew the lump was gone! Why would you spend money you don't have to confirm that?"

"Because she's my baby. I can't ignore my baby." Denise blew kisses at Blanca, who looked adorable sitting in her car seat.

Savannah said, "Okay, don't worry about the steaks, just come as you are this weekend."

"Thanks, but I just remembered, I've got to work. There's a band playing that I love so it should be fun. When these guys play..."

While Savannah listened to her sister, Jesus appeared sitting at the dining table. Excited to see him, she interrupted Denise, "Well, I hope you have a great weekend. I'll talk to you later. Bye."

The abrupt ending to their conversation surprised Denise, who asked Blanca, "I wonder what that was about?"

The furry princess tilted her head.

The Fiat drove down the scenic streets lined with historic houses while the woman talked to her dog about the band she loved and its handsome drummer. And, of course, Blanca hung onto every word.

Jesus and Savannah walked along the shore. The pier was just ahead. The tourists hung their fishing lines over the rail while seagulls tried to steal their bait.

"Do you have any questions regarding our journey to the stars and moon?" Jesus asked.

Savannah answered, "I know I should, but it seemed so natural. It was one of the first things in my life that really made sense, yet, I know that logically, or at least by the world's standards, it doesn't."

"Indeed. Trusting your inner guidance is one of the most difficult lessons there is."

Savannah offered an observation, "Ever notice that every time someone starts following their inner guidance, someone else kills them?" She listed names, "Gandhi, Martin Luther King Junior, the Kennedy brothers, John Lennon...the singer..." She trailed off, trying to think of another example.

Jesus said, "The world doesn't want to wake up. When someone starts to realize their true self, it scares those who aren't ready. You might remember that I was persecuted as well."

Savannah was embarrassed by her oversight. "I still don't understand why the Son of God had to die for our sins. Couldn't God just forgive us?"

"First, let me say that I am the Son of God, and you are his daughter. We are all created by the Father. Second, the purpose of the crucifixion was not to absolve your sins. The spirit has no sins. You cannot alter what God has created. The purpose of the crucifixion was to demonstrate there is no death."

Jesus continued, "How someone sees the crucifixion, or any event, depends on their state of mind. Once you are fully healed, you will realize that nothing but love is real. Then all thoughts of pain, fear and death, and even sin, will disappear."

Savannah bent over to pick up a cream-colored seashell. Bits of sand clung to it as she admired its beauty in the palm of her hand. Jesus cupped his hand under hers. The shell glowed, emitting streams of light. Savannah was mesmerized by its brilliance, as well as the connection she felt with it and Jesus.

Without taking her eyes away from the shell, she asked him, "How can something dead seem to have life coming out of it?"

"It's not dead. Nothing is dead. The power of God is in everything. You just have to look beyond the form. The form limits your ability to know the love that exists within. You were communicating with the stars and moon a few days ago. You should know this."

Jesus removed his hand. The light faded. The shell once again appeared ordinary.

"If I can't feel the love, why bother to know it's there?" She sounded discouraged.

"You will know eternal love. Everyone will. If not today, then someday. I promise you."

Savannah said, "Sorry to change the subject, but I want to get back to the dream...again. I know it's getting to be an old story, but it's constantly on my mind."

"Let's sit and discuss it."

They sat in the sand facing the ocean, the white-tipped waves rushing over the shore, creating a salty haze in the air.

Jesus said, "First, let me say that this dream is a gift. It's showing you the fear that resides within your mind. A fear that needs to be healed."

"I don't understand what you mean."

Jesus explained, "When mankind first believed he had been banished from God, he felt fear for the first time. Before that, you knew only eternal love. In this great void, you wondered if your ties to all of Creation had been severed. Perhaps forever."

"When you say 'mankind', do you mean all of us have this fear?"

"Yes."

"Then why aren't we aware of it?"

"The fear resides deep within your unconscious mind—purposely hidden by you because it is too horrific for you to face. Instead, you project the fear outward. All the undesirable events in your life are a projection of your fears—with most blamed on someone else. Or the weather. Or God. More specifically, your troublesome dream is a projection of your fears—spooned out in a dose you can mentally handle."

Jesus suggested, "Why don't we tour the dream you've been having, together? You can face it with me by your side, then you will know you are safe."

"Now?"

"If you wish."

"I don't think I can face watching the accident."

"What can you face?"

Savannah thought about Jesus' suggestion. Something had to be done. The dream wasn't going away on its own. She replied, "Take me to the Rosewood Center."

Jesus held out his hand.

Savannah took it.

Immediately, she was transported to where her other self was napping on a bed. Used tissues were scattered across the covers.

Jesus silently said to her, *Pay attention to how you feel when you know it's a dream.*

Savannah stared at her other self for a little while, but it seemed pointless to watch herself sleep. *Can we visit the rest of the facilities?*

Of course.

The two of them appeared on the courtyard. Savannah scanned the patients sitting there. They seemed oblivious to her and Jesus' presence.

Then she thought of Dr. Martin, and instantly they were transported to his office. The psychiatrist was meeting with another patient. Savannah didn't want to eavesdrop. Conflicted on where to go next, she stood there aimlessly.

It is your dream. What would you like to do? Jesus asked.

Can we visit the gravesites?

Of course.

They arrived at the cemetery, facing three gray granite tombstones. The one on the end was the largest. Savannah stared at the twin hearts etched with her and Steve's names. The date under hers was blank. On the two smaller stones, one was engraved with the name Justin and the other with Emily.

Savannah dropped to her knees, overcome with grief.

"Don't make it real," Jesus reminded her. "It's just a dream."

She admitted, "I guess I'm afraid this will really happen."

"I brought you here to face your fears, not reinforce them."

Emily and Justin appeared out of thin air.

Savannah was surprised by her children's unexpected arrival. She cried with joy, "Oh, I am so glad you're here! And alive!"

Emily looked at the tombstones, complaining, "How come Justin's stone is closest to yours? I'm the oldest!"

"Really? That's the first thing you noticed?" her mother asked.

Justin looked around the cemetery. "This is really creepy. Let's go, Emily."

The two of them vanished.

"Wow, that was surreal," Savannah commented. "Dreams are always so weird."

Trying to vanquish her fears, she sat on the grass beside the fresh mounds, watching the clouds float by. "Just let the dream go? That seems so easy, yet..."

She heard her daughter's voice calling from a distance, "Mom!"

Salty air blew over Savannah, creating a haze. When it dissipated, she found herself back at the beach, sitting in the sand beside Jesus.

Her children stood there staring down at them. The wind whipped Emily's hair and Justin's oversized t-shirt.

At first, Savannah was grateful to see them alive and well, but then her motherly instincts kicked in. "What are you doing out here by yourselves?"

"You were gone so long, we got worried," Emily told her. "We didn't know you were with Jesus or we wouldn't have."

Savannah saw her children's enthusiasm wane as their mini-adventure soured. She didn't want to spend this precious time scolding her children so instead she suggested, "Why don't we go eat at a restaurant on the beach? We can walk over after I grab some money."

The kids' smiles returned.

She asked Jesus, "Care to join us?"

"I would be honored."

They walked along the shore. Jesus' robe flowed majestically in the sea breeze. Savannah put her arm around Emily while Justin picked up seashells, throwing them back into the ocean.

CHAPTER 19

Two-week Extension

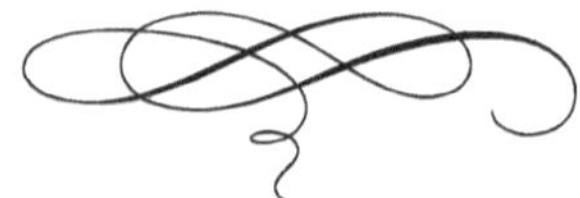

CAROL, HERMAN AND DENISE sat in Dr. Martin's office to discuss Savannah's condition.

The psychiatrist began the meeting by saying, "Thank you all for coming here. I have evaluated Savannah's mental status, and I have to say, her progress has been slower than anticipated. And although, in so many ways, she seems fine, she still believes this life is a dream. This hallucination probably began during her induced coma. As you know, some patients can have vivid dreams that seem very real to them. It can take weeks or even months to convince them otherwise."

"So we may have caused her delusions?" Denise asked, her voice tainted with guilt.

"Considering the pain and fragile state she was in, I

believe you made the best decision you could at the time. And yes, it may have had some serious side effects, but she'll get through this."

Dr. Martin continued, "Usually, after this length of time, I would recommend an out-patient facility, but, the reason you are here today is because I'm recommending that Savannah extend her time here at Rosewood so she can continue her sessions with me."

Herman expressed his opinion, "I think we should send her home, instead of hiding her away here. Maybe the familiar setting will help her realize she's not dreaming. She can always visit a therapist."

Carol chimed in, "If she went home now, who is going to drive her to rehab appointments and therapy sessions? I could help out, but not every day. I have to take care of my mother, who isn't doing well."

"I could do it every day," he stated. "I'm retired and can't think of anything better to do than take care of my daughter when she needs me."

Carol said with a mock-sweet voice and tight smile, "I've been driving you here. I don't think you're in good enough health to be taking care of someone else."

An irritated Dr. Martin tapped his fingers on his desk. He had given his professional opinion and nobody had paid any attention to it. He finally spoke up, proposing,

"How about a compromise? Let's extend her time here another two weeks. It's not nearly long enough, but I'll meet with her every day, and create a plan for her follow-up care. This will give you time to prepare."

"Two weeks is too long. Let's only extend it a week," Herman demanded.

Denise looked at her father, touching him on the arm, "Dad, Savannah isn't ready. None of us are, and we have a lot to figure out. Let's go with two weeks."

Herman fought back his tears. "Okay," he agreed.

After the session ended, the family went to Savannah's room to visit her.

Herman knocked on the door.

A woman's voice called out, "Come in!"

Denise punched the code into the keypad.

They all went inside.

Savannah was watching reruns of the game show "Jeopardy!" with Garret Barnes, the young man she had met on the courtyard. She shouted at the television, "Who is Judy Garland?"

"Who?" Garret asked her.

"It's before your time...Hey! Hello everybody," Savannah greeted her family, who stood awkwardly at the edge of the living area. "Have you met Garret yet?"

She didn't wait for their response, "Dad, Carol, Denise, this is Garret. He's another patient here."

Herman stepped closer, shaking the young man's hand. Carol and Denise said hello to him.

Garret sensed Savannah needed to be alone with her family so he excused himself, saying he had a rehabilitation appointment, then left the room using his new crutches.

The door closed.

"So, how are you feeling?" Carol inquired.

Savannah answered, "Better. The pain is finally subsiding."

"That's good. Well, we just met with Dr. Martin to discuss when you should go home."

Home? Savannah asked herself. *There's no home here. Not in this dream.* She chose her words carefully because she had become very aware of how much her statements about life being a dream scared everyone. "I'm not ready to go home," she said firmly.

Carol gently responded, "It's okay, honey. It'll be a few weeks before that happens. We just wanted you to get mentally prepared. And, once you're home, we can help you to your doctor appointments and such."

Savannah felt the fear rise up in her stomach. *What if I'm trapped in this dream?* she wondered. *I should have woken up by now.* She looked at their faces, the same faces that in her real life brought her such comfort, but here, she felt they were trying to trick her into believing this dream's reality. "I guess you've got it all figured out," she said with a tone that betrayed her anger.

Carol looked at Herman to see if he had any ideas on how to remedy the situation, but he avoided her gaze. They all wanted this ordeal to be over so they could return to their normal lives, but they all knew nothing would ever be the same, especially for Savannah.

CHAPTER 20

The Card

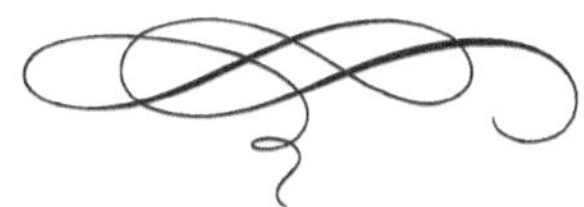

"YOU'RE DRIVING TOO CLOSE to that car," Herman stated nervously.

Carol remained silent. She had clearly reached the limit of her patience with him.

"Aren't you going to slow down?"

Carol gritted her teeth, but kept her composure, thinking to herself, *Only a few more minutes before we reach his house. I can make it that far.*

"Would you mind stopping at the drugstore up there?" Herman asked. "I have a prescription to pick up."

"Would you like to go inside and browse around as well?" she asked sarcastically.

"Actually, there is something I would like to get."

Carol regretted her insincere offer.

After parking, Herman struggled to get out of the car, then they both went inside. The pharmacy was at the rear of the store.

At the counter, after being informed that his order wasn't ready, Herman complained to Carol, "Bet they didn't even start on it until I got here. Why bother to call ahead?"

She couldn't take it anymore, and told him she needed to look at some things on the other side of the store.

Left alone, Herman ambled over to the card aisle. He browsed through the sympathy cards, but decided it was too late for that sentiment, then he looked at the "cheer someone up" cards. *Nope, that's not it*, he thought. Finally, he found just the right card.

Herman returned to the pharmacy's waiting area, sitting in one of the chairs along the wall.

A few minutes later, Carol returned, asking him if he was ready to go.

"Nope. Still waiting. Did you find what you were looking for?"

"No, they didn't have it," she fibbed, sitting beside him. It was then she noticed the card in his hand with the word "daughter" printed in large script letters. Her heart softened, knowing how helpless Herman must feel after his recent heart attack, combined with the grief of losing their loved ones and, not to mention, Savannah's unstable mental condition.

Without saying another word, the two of them waited for his order to be filled.

CHAPTER 21

Telling Garret

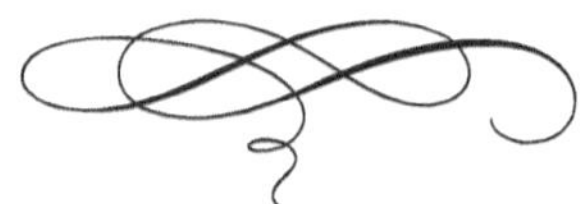

SAVANNAH LOUNGED ON THE courtyard with Garret, enjoying the warmth of the day. Her wheelchair had been replaced with a walker.

"I'm going home tomorrow," Garret mentioned. If it weren't for the cane, he would have looked perfectly healthy.

"I have to leave in a few days myself." Savannah's apprehension was clearly visible on her face.

"I'll miss our talks and 'Jeopardy!' dates." He had said it as a joke, but he really would miss her.

Savannah admired how handsome Garret looked as he leaned his muscular arm on the table. A tattoo peeked out from beneath his t-shirt sleeve. She was surprised at how comfortable she felt around him, especially considering their age difference.

"Savannah, I hope you don't mind me asking, but, all the time you've been here, I've never seen your husband or kids visit you. Were they hurt in the car accident?"

"No. They're alive and well. They're just not here."

"Where are they?"

"At the beach house."

"But surely they would visit you!" Garret exclaimed in disbelief.

"They can't."

"Why not?"

"It's hard to explain."

"Try me."

"You wouldn't understand."

"Probably not, but I'd like to think you could confide in me."

"You really want to know?"

"Look, I'll be gone after today. What have you got to lose?"

Savannah gathered her courage, then revealed her story, "Here, in this life, I've lost my family in a car accident."

The enormity of her situation hit Garret like a ton of bricks.

She continued, "But it's all right, because it's just a

dream. When I'm awake, in my real life, I'm with my family at the beach, and this is just a bad dream a few times a week."

Garret leaned in closer, putting his arms around her. His touch caused a rush of emotions to swell within Savannah. She began to cry, pressing her face into his chest.

He stroked the back of her head, whispering, "It's all right. It's all right."

Her cries turned into sobs and her whole body shook. He gently rocked her. Garret couldn't imagine how much pain she was in, but he could understand her wanting to believe this life wasn't real.

CHAPTER 22

Dreams within Dreams

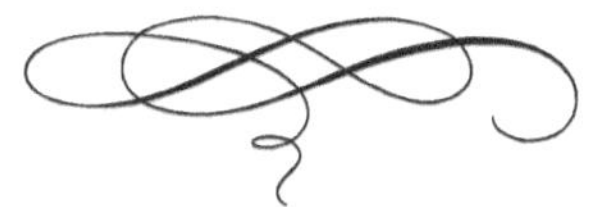

IT WAS SUNDAY EVENING. The family had already eaten dinner, and soon would be heading home.

The kids were playing with their phones.

Steve was watching a football game he had recorded.

Savannah walked alone on the beach, enjoying the last rays of sunlight, wearing a jacket to protect herself against the chilly wind. She found a dry spot on the sand, sitting down, pulling the jacket over her knees. Sandpipers ran along the shore probing for food, emitting their distinct high-pitched bird calls as they avoided the waves, dashing back and forth in a comical dance with the ocean.

Jesus appeared sitting beside Savannah.

She felt his presence. Without looking at him, she

said, "The dream hasn't stopped. I thought after you gave me the tour, it would have. Is there something else I need to know?"

"The fact that the dream bothers you means you still believe in its reality."

"Is it real?"

"No."

His quick answer made Savannah think of another possibility. She asked, "Is this life real?"

"No."

She shrieked, "These are both a dream!?"

Jesus waited for her to calm down, then stated, "Life is a dream. It is an elaborate creation of your own imagination. A projection of your mind that is mostly fueled by your fears. You even have dreams within dreams, such as those at night. Your creative powers are endless."

Savannah countered, "There's no mention of life being a dream in the Bible."

"It was written that Adam fell into a deep sleep, but nowhere does it say he woke up."

"But you're awake," she pointed out.

Jesus said, "I should clarify that you are awake. You simply think you are dreaming."

"So, if it's my dream, can I change it?"

"Of course, you can. You were created in God's likeness, and you have all the power of your Creator. When you give up your fears, you will awaken to the eternal love that surrounds you. Your dreams of dying will turn into dreams of heaven. Then God will take the final step to welcome you home."

CHAPTER 23

Take My Hand

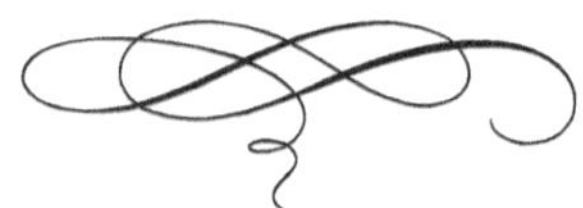

NIGHT HAD COME AT the Rosewood Rehabilitation Center. Savannah sat in bed staring at the full moon through the window, feeling desperate and alone, especially since Garret had been discharged. She wondered what her other self was doing. Was she home from the beach? Having a glass of wine before bed? Had she eaten steak earlier? Savannah silently screamed at her other self, *Get me out of this nightmare!*

Yet she remained captive in the shadows.

Savannah got out of bed, using the walker to reach the window, placing her hand against the glass, eclipsing the moon, beckoning her other self with her bitter thoughts. *We share the same moon. Two souls on opposite sides of a mirror. Mine is a dark reflection, twisted and distorted through a pane of glass that doesn't even exist while you live in the light.* She implored out loud, "Can you hear me? Can you see me? Wake up, Savannah! Wake up!"

There was no response.

She hobbled back to bed, pulling the covers over her shivering body, sensing an impending doom. The mirror was falling, and its dark glass was about to shatter into a million pieces—forever severing the portal between their realities and leaving her stuck here, forgotten in this nightmare.

Suddenly, Jesus appeared beside her bed.

She sat up. For the first time since this ordeal began, she had hope.

"You're not forgotten," Jesus said gently.

Savannah pleaded, "I want out of this nightmare. Will you help me?"

Jesus said to her, "Take my hand."

And she did.

CHAPTER 24

Dreams of Heaven

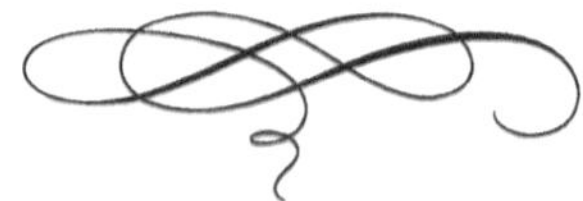

AT THE BEACH HOUSE, Savannah tossed and turned in her sleep. She heard the dream's familiar sounds of rain, idling engines and voices.

A bright light flashed in her eyes, momentarily blinding her before jolting her awake.

A paramedic rushed toward her.

Rain dripped inside the car through the gaping holes. She could smell the earth's moist poignant scents of both life and decay, rising from its humus sanctuary.

Through the mist, Samson, their beloved Labrador, strolled out of the woods. He quickened his pace as he neared his mistress, wagging his tail.

Savannah turned toward her husband. He smiled at her with a love so intense that the car's interior was barely discernible behind his glorious light. She turned around to look at the backseat, gazing with wonder at Emily and Justin who radiated golden rays that extended to the heavens. *You all look so beautiful!* she thought joyfully.

The paramedic shouted, "We're losing her!"

Savannah didn't hear him. She was too busy admiring her family's angelic faces and feeling the love that ebbed and flowed between them and the entire universe. She wondered how she could have ever believed in death.

The wreckage vanished into the loving light.

Savannah and Steve each took hold of their children's hands, leaving the dream together.

About the Author

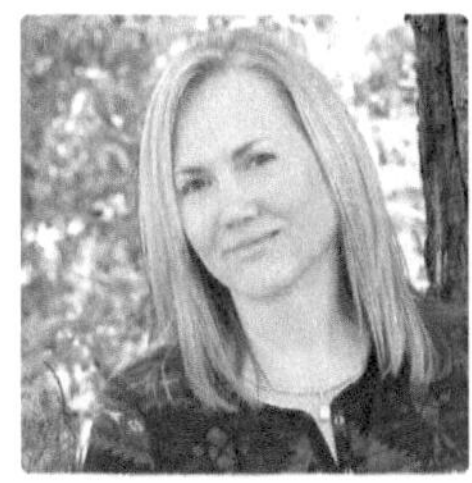 ELIZABETH M. HERRERA is a shamanic healer and author of life-changing books. Her stories encourage people to stretch outside their comfort zones and reexamine their own beliefs.

She inherited her rebellious spirit from her father who was raised by his grandfather–a full-blooded Apache who smuggled sugar and flour from Mexico into Texas, exchanged gunfire with Texas Rangers and crossed paths with Pancho Villa.

Elizabeth was raised in a Christian home, but lost her faith in her early twenties. For over a decade, she searched for something to fill the void, eventually discovering Native American spirituality. Through this spiritual practice, she unexpectedly became a catalyst for healing and miracles. These events led her back to a belief in a higher power.

Elizabeth is the author of the books *Shaman Stone Soup* (Memoir, Spirituality), *Earth Sentinels: The Storm Creators* (Contemporary Fantasy), and *Of Stars and Clay,* (Science Fiction, Fantasy, Dystopian).